学术写作十讲

杜垚 著

Ten Lectures on Academic Writing

北京大学出版社
PEKING UNIVERSITY PRESS

图书在版编目(CIP)数据

学术写作十讲 / 杜垚著. —— 北京：北京大学出版社, 2025.1. —— ISBN 978-7-301-35648-7

Ⅰ. H052

中国国家版本馆 CIP 数据核字第 2024PU1728 号

书　　　　名	学术写作十讲 XUESHU XIEZUO SHI JIANG
著作责任者	杜　垚　著
责 任 编 辑	朱房煦
标 准 书 号	ISBN 978-7-301-35648-7
出 版 发 行	北京大学出版社
地　　　　址	北京市海淀区成府路 205 号　100871
网　　　　址	http://www.pup.cn　　新浪微博: @北京大学出版社
电 子 邮 箱	编辑部 pupwaiwen@pup.cn　总编室 zpup@pup.cn
电　　　　话	邮购部 010-62752015　发行部 010-62750672 编辑部 010-62754382
印 刷 者	河北博文科技印务有限公司
经 销 者	新华书店 650 毫米×980 毫米　16 开本　21 印张　305 千字 2025 年 1 月第 1 版　　2025 年 1 月第 1 次印刷
定　　　　价	78.00 元

未经许可，不得以任何方式复制或抄袭本书之部分或全部内容。
版权所有，侵权必究
举报电话: 010-62752024　电子邮箱: fd@pup.cn
图书如有印装质量问题，请与出版部联系，电话: 010-62756370

序

《学术写作十讲》成书过程中,杜垚博士便嘱我写序。我又惊又喜:惊的是岁月飞逝,喜的是卓越成长。2010年,我在北京外国语大学中国外语教育研究中心从事博士后研究工作,一个偶然的机会,成了杜垚的硕士学位论文指导教师。那时她的学术能力就十分出色,积极思考、善于发现问题、不断创新、勇于实践,展现出巨大的学术潜力。我很幸运能见证她的学术成长。硕士毕业,她便考取了博士,继续自己的学术生涯。12年过去了,她的新作《学术写作十讲》再次展现了她独特的视角、扎实的学养和亲切的风格。

在我看来,现有的学术英语写作著作大体可分为两类。一类按照学术论文的篇章结构讲解英语写作,另一类按照学术论文的写作过程讲解英语写作。这两类著作虽各有特色和优势,但弊端也十分明显——初学者无法通过掌握篇章结构或写作过程去掌握学术英语写作技能。事实上,学术论文是"做"出来的,不是"写"出来的。对于初涉学术研究的新手而言,他们的实践经验甚少,直接学习专业期刊中的学术文章,也只能了解写作技术层面的皮毛,无法理解他人行文背后的写作和思考原则。写作过程虽说步骤大体相同,但并非一个线性流程。所以,初学者同样也很难通过了解流程提升学术写作技能。此外,这两类著作的写作风格通常是正式严肃的,虽然也划分成不同分册来体现难度进阶,但通常无法有针对性地回应初学者面临的实际问题。因此,使用者往往觉得相关著作不接地气,实用价值低。

  面对上述弊端,我认为需要从学术写作新手的实际问题出发,以他们急需掌握的核心能力为抓手,用他们容易理解的方式讲述学术写作。杜垚博士的《学术写作十讲》恰恰就是按照这个思路展开的。该书的十讲依次是:读者—论证—组织—流动—炼句—用词—征引—数据—工具—日常。单看这些讲次的名称就有令人耳目一新的感觉。它们覆盖了学术写作初学者最需要掌握的核心技能。例如,明确目标读者、提出自己的论点、整合论点与论据、采用流畅的衔接手段、使用准确的词语和句式、恰当引用他人文献、有效呈现和解释数据、合理借助写作工具、发展适合自身的学术英语写作策略等。这种设计的最大优势在于,它从学习者需求出发,想学习者之所想,急学习者之所急。读者可以根据自己的实际需求直奔相关讲次,了解所需知识,掌握相关技能。该书还为读者推荐了学术写作书籍以及网络资源。

  此外,该书十分便于学术英语教师使用。当前我国学术英语教学的实际状况是，专业背景不同的学生往往处在同一课堂听英语专业背景出身的教师讲授学术英语。如果以某一专业的学术文章为例，其他专业的学生未必获益，且任课教师会因为缺乏相关专业知识觉得教学实操难度大。这时，最佳的做法便是抽取所有专业学生所必需的学术英语技能作为训练核心，由教师引导加以训练。《学术写作十讲》就是按照这种思路设计和编写的。因此，英语专业背景出身的语言教师完全可以参考这本著作面向各个专业的学术英语初学者进行授课。这既解决了语言教师专业知识缺乏时的尴尬处境，又使所有学生的学习效果最大化。《学术写作十讲》既可以独立使用，也可以作为配套资源与相关学术英语教材联合使用。这给予任课教师很大的灵活性。

该书的第三个优势，也是我特别赞同和推崇的，就是它的讲述式行文风格。《学术写作十讲》各讲次均以任课教师向学生讲述的口吻展开。读者阅读本书时，就仿佛有一位老师正在将相关知识娓娓道来，而这些知识恰好又是读者最想获得的。讲述过程中，作者巧妙地将学术英语写作的有关理论、经典研究、典型案例融入进来，让读者在不知不觉中掌握学术写作原理，同时通过实例体会这些原理的实际应用。每讲之后的练习少而精，与各讲主题及关键能力十分契合。这种风格让读者感觉轻松、愉快。他们没有被说教、被灌输、被约束的感觉，而是在温馨、平等、自由的氛围中学习相关知识和技能。

《学术写作十讲》的设计非常独特，使它在同类书籍中脱颖而出。多年来，我一直从事学术英语写作教学工作，也一直在寻找适用面更广、对学生更有帮助、教师更容易使用的教学材料。杜垚博士的这本新作刚好满足了我的期待。我也相信,它能为更多的师生带来启发和帮助。

许宏晨

北京语言大学

2022 年 12 月

写在前面的话

在中国科学院大学第一次讲授"英文学术写作"这门课时,我请同学们用一句话来描述对学术写作的感受。在我收到的回答里,出现最多的是:

学术写作是困难的。(Academic writing is difficult.)

具体的困难之处,来自面对不熟悉的文体:

学术写作真的与我十几年写作文的经历不同,以前最爱写散文,夹杂着写些议论文、记叙文。所以刚开始写论文的时候,文章写得很散,导师说读起来"像写作文似的"。(ZF,环境工程专业)

来自对语言不能准确表达思想的担忧：

我认为学术写作像是编写算法，算法中每一条指令都有明确含义，而学术论文中每一句话也应当准确无误地传达作者的观点。然而，有时候我反复思考和推敲，仍然难以找到合适的表达方式。"所想"和"所写"之间似乎总存在着无形的 gap。（Vince，人工智能专业）

来自在浩瀚文献中找不到自己的声音：

For me, writing a thesis is a process of planting a tree in a forest. Stepping into the forest, its vastness strikes my heart, so numerous are the plants that I find myself voiceless and lost. Though gradually I find some voices, they overlap with forerunners. To have a place, it is necessary for me to make a distinction between me and others. In this process, self-doubt comes to me as well. I wonder if I can really plant my own tree in this forest.（XXY，英国文学专业）

我试着问学生们：学术写作有没有简单和容易的部分？教室内鸦雀无声。许久，有同学小心翼翼地说：或许结构是相对简单的？学术写作感觉有一定的规律。

这是很好的直觉。我鼓励同学们继续思考，试着跳出学术写作的框框，和其他类型的写作比一比，甚至和其他的创造性活动比一比。同学们你一言，我一语，从中又发现了不少学术写作相对简单和容易的部分。

> 写小说需要构建一个合理的虚拟世界，散文需要美，这些都需要写作本身的变化，需要不落俗套。学术写作是科学研究的文字载体，不需要过多的创新。

> 已经发表出来的东西就摆在那里了，总可以依葫芦画瓢。

> 学术写作可以反复修改，一直改到自己满意为止。不像画画，比如一张国画，一旦落笔，就要接受水墨的随机性。

你看，仅仅是泡一壶茶的功夫，我们就跳出了在"困难"这个框架下思考学术写作，关注到了它相对"容易""简单"的方面。

学术写作不那么强调修辞和文采，这个"易"的反面就是学术写作对精确性、逻辑性要求极高的"难"；学术写作有那么多可供学习、借鉴的模本，这个"易"的反面就是学术写作不容忍抄袭，对原创性要求极高的"难"；学术写作可以反复修改，这个"易"的反面就是我们要接受终稿不完美的"难"。可见，难易相倚、相生、相成。难和易本就是统一的。

关于同学们对学术写作的感受，我还收到了这样的回答：

在学术写作时，我总是觉得孤独。

学术写作是个漫长的历程，一篇文章从写作到发表少则数月，长则数年。这种文体似乎又要求我们退居幕后、隐藏自我、追求客观。想象一下数码相机产生以前要在暗室里冲洗照片的胶卷时代，我们是不是能在小黑屋里待上很久？孤独感在这个过程中产生，实在是再正常不过的事。

我也曾在黑暗中摸索着完成了人生的第一篇英文论文，但投稿之后一年的经历更新了我的认知：学术写作并不孤独。我们以往的写作（无论母语还是外语），得到一个分数和几句评语，往往意味着一次写作的终结；而当学术文章写就，通常会经历一个同行评审的过程。这是我们从小到大都很陌生的体验。审稿人通常会对文章的价值和不足给出很具体的评价，提供详尽的修改建议，对已完成的修改给出反馈。在一轮又一轮的修改中，我们得以与学术共同体对话，逐渐熟悉本学科的话语体系。

而最终发表出来的文章，看上去是个体或团队独立的劳动成果，实则凝聚了很多人的心血，也代表了集体智慧所能达到的一种高度。

还想提到一个我印象很深的表述：

英语不是我们的母语。用英语写作，我们一点优势也没有。

用不是母语的一门外语从事学术写作的确不容易。课上的同学们曾用一些生动的比喻表达了对英文写作的看法。

> 英文写作就像是用非利手去吃面条，可以吃完也可以吃饱，但是吃的过程总是不那么舒心。

> 英文写作就像是行走在刚刚结冰的湖面上，只能小心翼翼地试探，没有脚踏实地的感觉。

> 英文写作就像是不懂穿衣搭配，看到一个人穿了件羽绒服很好看，另一个人穿了一件短裤很好看，我们就将羽绒服和短裤搭配在一起出门了。

我们或许都曾为自己英文写作中的二语写作者身份感到过困扰。在一次学术会议中，肯·海兰德（Ken Hyland）教授的一席话对我有很大启发。他说，在学术写作中，没有母语者和非母语者的区别，只有专家写作者和新手写作者的差别。后来我常常想到这句话，它于朴素之中有一些莫名其妙的、鼓舞人心的力量。

那么，专家写作者和新手写作者的差别到底是什么呢？当学生能写出基本通顺且合乎语法的句子后，经过了严格学术写作训练到底意味着什么呢？学术写作是可教的吗？学术写作中哪些技能经过学习可以获得明显的进步，而哪些功夫的提升非经历岁月不可？

这些问题，在备课、上课、批阅学生的课程论文时会经常浮现在我的脑海。我把对这些问题的思考慢慢地写成了文字，于是有了这样一本基于课堂讲义的《学术写作十讲》。

本书第一至六讲为读者、论证、组织、流动、炼句和用词。这六讲的次序安排意在说明：写学术文章，整体的读者定位、行文逻辑和组织运思要先于局部的选词炼句和流畅通达；第七、八讲两讲为征引和数据。征引是学术文章的显著特征，正确而有效地征引他人文献在学术写作中至关重要。同样重要的，还有数据评述，这类写作多用于需要亲自采集数据的实证性文章。读者可以把第七、八讲两讲和前面六讲并置起来，当作一个相对独立的单元来学习，也可以把这两讲融入前六讲大的体系之中，思考征引与数据在文章整体的论证中起到了怎样的作用。第九讲介绍了学术写作的工具，第十讲介绍了写作的心法，一个是向外所求，一个是向内所求，一个是真效率，一个是慢功夫。每讲后面的练习，取自给学生布置的课后作业，书后附学生作业的示例供读者参考。

这门课已经教了很多年，越教越有劲头，我想这功劳在学术写作本身。它让我们有机会接近和成为知识的源头，并在源头活水的浸润中，成为独一无二的自己。

杜 垚

2022 年岁末

目 录

001 第一讲　读者

037 第二讲　论证

067 第三讲　组织

085 第四讲　流动

105 第五讲　炼句

129 第六讲　用词

157 第七讲　征引

183 第八讲　数据

205 第九讲　工具

227 第十讲　日常

247 参考答案

| 307 | 学术写作资源 |
| 319 | 后　记 |

第一讲　读　者

这一讲，我们谈谈学术写作中的读者意识。

先来看一个具体的例子。

心理学上有一个很著名的实验，叫作"棉花糖实验"。这是20世纪60年代斯坦福大学的心理学家沃尔特·米歇尔（Walter Mischel）和他的同事开展的有关自控力的一系列实验。他们试图找到人在幼年时期的自控力水平和成年后人生成就的关联。这一长达数年的实验在心理学领域产生了深远的影响。

下面我们先来看看介绍这个实验的两个版本。第一个版本[①]来自米歇尔教授的专著，书名就叫《棉花糖实验》，第二个版本[②]来自大家都很熟悉的《科学》杂志，作者也是米歇尔本人。这两个版本在字数上相差无几，请大家仔细阅读，看看内容上有哪些不同。

---

① MISCHEL W. The marshmallow test: Mastering self-control ［M］. New York: Little, Brown Spark, 2004: 5.

② MISCHEL W, SHODA Y, RODRIGUEZ M L. Delay of gratification in children ［J］. Science, 1989, 244 (4907): 933-938.

版本一（来自科普专著《棉花糖实验》）

It began in the 1960s with preschoolers at Stanford University's Bing Nursery School, in a simple study that challenged them with a tough dilemma. My students and I gave the children a choice between one reward (for example, a marshmallow) that they could have immediately, and a larger reward (two marshmallows) for which they would have to wait, alone, for up to 20 minutes. We let the children select the rewards they wanted most from an assortment that included marshmallows, cookies, little pretzels, mints, and so on. "Amy," for example, chose marshmallows. She sat alone at a table facing the one marshmallow that she could have immediately, as well as the two marshmallows that she could have if she waited. Next to the treats was a desk bell she could ring at any time to call back the researcher and eat the one marshmallow. Or she could wait for the researcher to return, and if Amy hadn't left her chair or started to eat the marshmallow, she could have both. The struggles we observed as these children tried to restrain themselves from ringing the bell could bring tears to your eyes, have you applauding their creativeness and cheering them on, and give you fresh hope for the potential of even young children to resist temptation and persevere for their delayed rewards.

版本二（来自《科学》杂志）

In this method, the experimenter begins by showing the child some toys, explaining they will play with them later (so that ending the delay leads to uniform positive consequences). Next, the experimenter teaches a game in which he or she has to leave the room and comes back immediately when the child summons by ringing a bell. Each child then is shown a pair of treats (such as snacks, small toys, or tokens) which differ in value, established through pretesting to bedesirable and of age-appropriate interest (for example, one marshmallow versus two; two small cookies versus five pretzels). The children are told that to attain the one they prefer they have to wait until the experimenter returns but that they are free to end the waiting period whenever they signal; if they do, however, they will get the less preferred object and forgo the other one. The items in the pair are selected to be sufficiently close in value to create a conflict situation for young children between the temptation to stop

> the delay and the desire to persist for the preferred outcome when the latter requires delay. After children understand the contingency, they are left on their own during the delay period while their behavior is observed unobtrusively, and the duration of their delay is recorded until they terminate or the experimenter returns (typically after 15 minutes).

不知道大家有没有和我相似的感觉：第一个版本故事性更强、叙述更生动，我们很容易就被带到了这个挺吸引人的实验里。作者在段落的中间部分举了艾米（Amy）的例子。例子的使用增强了代入感，使抽象的实验步骤显得可见可感。第二个版本似乎欠生动，但时间线更清晰，对细节的交代也更多。比如，从第二个版本中，我们得知，实验并不是一上来就告知孩子们两种选择是什么，在这之前，实验者给孩子们展示了若干玩具，承诺会在"游戏"结束后陪他们一起玩，还给孩子讲了这个"游戏"的玩法。

下面我们再看看心理学专业期刊《人格与社会心理学杂志》是如何介绍这个实验的。① 这篇文章很长，限于篇幅，我仅给大家展示其中的一段。

---

① MISCHEL W, EBBESEN E B. Attention in delay of gratification [J]. Journal of Personality and Social Psychology, 1970, 16(2): 329-337.

版本三（节选自专业期刊）

Subjects and Experimenters

The subjects were 16 boys and 16 girls attending the Bing Nursery School of Standford University. Three other subjects were run but eliminated because of their failure to comprehend the instructions as described later. The children ranged in age from 3 years, 6 months, to 5 years, 8 months (with a median age of 4 years, 6 months). The procedures were conducted by two male experimenters. Eight subjects (4 males and 4 females) were assigned randomly to each of the four experimental conditions. In each condition each experimenter ran 2 males and 2 females in order to avoid systematic biasing effects from sex or experimenters.

就实验参与者来说，从之前两个版本中，我们仅读到了 preschoolers/child。这种表述提供的被试信息极少。具体有多少个孩子参与？性别如何？年龄是一样的吗？这些信息在第三个版本中有所呈现。不仅被试的情况有所交代，实验员的信息也清晰地呈现给了读者。如把这篇文章的 Methods 部分全部读完，你一定会赞叹作者在实验中若干细微之处的精心设计，比如作者完整记录了实验员对孩子说的话的脚本,在不同时间以不同方式反复确认孩子是否听懂了指令。通读完成后,我们会发现,这个实验似乎不是第一个版本描述的"simple study"那样简单。

以上三个版本都可以称作学术文体。可见,学术文体不是千篇一律,一成不变的。从科普专著到专业期刊,同一个实验呈现出来的面貌如此不同。在信息和细节的呈现上,不同的学术文体在一个两极中的连续体上做着选择。

如果用艺术史中的两幅画来表达这两极的特征的话,我想选用莫奈(1840—1926)的《日本桥》(图1-1)和古埃及墓室壁画《内巴蒙的花园》(图1-2)。

图1-1 《日本桥》
(1900)

图1-2 《内巴蒙的花园》
(约公元前14世纪)

同样是描绘自然美景,图1-1莫奈这座位于塞纳河畔吉维尼小镇的花园在光与影中显得非常炫目。花园中的碧波一眼望不到尽头,碧波中的睡莲虽然看不清轮廓,但在自然的光色变换中,让人感到浪漫的诗意,甚至有一丝梦幻的气息。观者很容易被画面吸引,如同我们很容易被版本一描述的那个棉花糖实验吸引一样。

相形之下,图 1-2《内巴蒙的花园》轮廓清晰、线条简单,甚至显出了几分稚拙之气。虽然粗看很难让人印象深刻,但细细看来,我们看到了方形池塘中的鱼儿、鸭子、白色的睡莲,也看到了池边的椰枣树、无花果树和槐树,不能不赞叹这花园的生机勃勃,枝繁叶茂。这幅画最有意思的地方,还在于它选取的视角。为了勾勒一个完整的池塘,画家选取了从天空俯视的上帝视角,由此我们有幸看到池塘的全貌。更有趣的是,池塘中的生物却都是平视的视角,仿佛出自小孩子的手笔。池塘边的树木视角也很独特,左边的三棵直接平躺了。可见,作者选取了最能体现事物特征的视角,试图清晰地表现出每一样事物的完整轮廓。

介绍棉花糖实验的第三个版本,就像这个《内巴蒙的花园》,初看似乎平淡无奇,作者只是一步一步地交代,先做了什么,后做了什么。但若细细分析着看,我们不难看出作者在设计实验时的精心,对若干细节的考虑。作者不介意把文章背后的一些细致的考虑交代给读者,而这许多细节,连同简洁的表达,形成了另一种意义上的印象深刻。

介绍棉花糖实验的三个版本并没有好坏优劣之分。三个版本不同的风貌,是米歇尔教授的一种主动选择,显示了其心中明晰的读者定位。

第一个版本是科普专著,通常面向学术领域外对心理学实验感兴趣的普通读者,也就是象牙塔外的大众。米歇尔教授在这本专著的序言中说:在《棉花糖实验》的写作过程中,我一直想象着自己正与您——我的读者进行一次悠闲的对话，就像与朋友和熟人的对话一样。对话发起于这样一个问题："棉花糖实验的研究有什么最新进展？"①

第二个版本发表于《科学》杂志，经常阅读这本杂志的多是受过基本科研训练的学者和学生，并不局限于心理学。比如这本杂志的读者可能是寻找跨领域合作可能性的学者。

第三个版本发表于心理学专业期刊，读者多是同领域的人士，也就是我们常说的同行。

读者意识的本质是一种共情能力，这是写作的一种底层能力。正如我们给他人送礼物时需要思考：别人是不是已经有了这样东西？他/她目前是不是需要这样东西？学术写作时，我们也需要自问：

1. 我们在与谁交流？谁是我们的目标读者？

2. 读者就这个话题已经有了哪些背景知识？

3. 读者期待从我们的文章中收获什么？

当我们心中有了读者意识之后，怎么通过不同的语言形式和风格，来展现不同的文体风貌呢？我们从以下五个方面，再来分析一下这三个版本。

（一）时间词

时间词的使用能清晰地表明实验步骤，增强行文的逻辑性。第一个版本中没有使用时间词，而第二、三个版本中用了不少的

---

① 沃尔特·米歇尔. 棉花糖实验：自控力养成圣经［M］. 任俊，同欢，译. 北京：北京联合出版公司，2016：XIII.

时间词。现举第二个版本中的几个例子：

In this method, the experimenter begins by showing…

Next, the experimenter teaches…

Each child then is shown a pair of treats…

After the children…, and the duration is their delay is recorded until they…

（二）意图性小句

为了能更好地向读者传达实验设计背后的意图，作者在第二、三个版本中都使用了意图性小句，而第一个版本中无此类小句。下面我们具体看看第三个版本的八个意图性小句。

小孩子能否理解他们要面临的两种选择，是整个实验成败的关键。因此，在版本三的八个意图性小句中，有三个是确定小孩子听懂了指令：

To ensure that the child learned reliably how to bring the experimenter back, this sequence was repeated four times…

… to assess if the subject understood them, the experimenter asked three questions…

To determine whether or not the child remembered the waiting contingencies when the experimenter finally returned, he asked the child, "What happens now?"

取得孩子的信任和配合，减少他们心里的焦虑，是实验顺利进展的另一个重要因素。三个意图性小句与此相关：

These nurturant sessions were designed <u>so that the children would more readily agree to accompany the experimenters to the "surprise room"</u> …

These references to the toys were designed <u>to help relax the children</u> …

This instruction was included <u>to stress that the child's waiting behavior would not affect his later play period in the surprise room</u>.

还有两个意图性小句和实验者有关，体现了整体设计背后考虑的因素：

In each condition each experimenter ran 2 males and 2 females <u>in order to avoid systematic biasing effects from sex or experimenters</u>.

This method <u>assured that the experimenter remained unaware of the subject's experimental condition until the last possible moment in the procedure</u>.

（三）人称

学术写作中，选取不同的人称，体现了不同的写作视角。以当事人的角度，使用第一人称，讲述如何一步步展开研究，会突显研究主体；以旁观者的角度，用第三人称讲述，具有弱化、隐藏研究主体的效果；而第二人称的使用，通常会拉近作者与读者的距离，将读者代入作者的叙述当中。

棉花糖实验的第一个版本用了第一人称，比如"My students and I gave…"，"We let the children…"，"The struggles we observed as these children…"。此外，通过第二人称 you/your 的使用，拉近了和读者的距离，比如"…could bring tears to your eyes, have you applauding their…, and give you fresh hope for…"。

第二和第三个版本没有选取第一人称，而是用了 experimenter 一词指称实验者。这两个版本也没有使用第二人称和读者产生关联。

（四）被动语态

通常来讲，被动语态的使用可以隐去动作的真正施动者，从某种程度上弱化人的因素对实验的影响，从而"增强"实验的客观性。如果将目光聚焦于语态的使用，我们会发现第一个版本没有一处使用被动语态，第二个版本的 6 句话里有 4 句话都用到了被动语态，第三个版本方法部分正文的 40 句话里面有 15 句话用到了被动语态。现举版本二中的几个例子：

> Each child is then shown …
>
> The children are told that …
>
> The items in the pair are selected to …

（五）选词

如果我问大家，以上三个版本中，哪个版本里生词更多，你一定会毫不犹豫地选择第二个或第三个。阅读中，你可能把一些不认识的词画线，比如 forgo，contingency，unobtrusively。另外，你会发现，在表达同一个意思时，版本二、三选取了比版本一看上去更正式的词。比如在叙述孩子们会"得到"何种奖励时，版本一使用了 have 一词，而版本三使用了更为正式的 attain。

My students and I gave the children a choice between one reward that they could <u>have</u> immediately, ...（版本一）

The children are told that to <u>attain</u> the one they prefer...（版本二）

再如呈现孩子们可以按铃"召唤"实验员这个信息时，版本一用的是短语 call back，而版本三用的是 summon 这一较为正式的词。

Next to the treats was a desk bell she could ring at any time to <u>call back</u> the researcher and eat the one marshmallow.（版本一）

The next phase required teaching the child the technique for terminating the waiting period and <u>summoning</u> the experimenter at will.（版本三）

以上五个方面不是面向不同读者写作的金科玉律，而是我们基于对事实的观察得出的一些规律。如果你仔细阅读这三个版本，可能会发现更多的不同。

我们可能还暂时做不到像米歇尔教授一样灵活地变通文字，但"心里有读者"的意识至关重要。不妨在写作时，从自己的作者身份中抽离出一个读者，从"他"或"她"的视角再看看自己写的文字。很多时候，让外行明白比让同行明白更难，因为我们和同行有相似的知识结构，有共同的术语表达；而让外行明白，往往需要我们整个知识大厦的根基十分牢固。

知识的大厦来自一砖一瓦，几千字的文章也来自一词一句。只要把知识的基础打牢、把写作的基本功练好，日后发表是顺其自然的事。棉花糖实验说的是一种延迟满足，学术研究和写作又何尝不是？

这一讲的最后，和大家分享王阳明《传习录》中的一段话。与大家共勉！

> 立志用功如种树然，方其根芽，犹未有干，及其有干，尚未有枝，枝而后叶，叶而后花实。初种根时，只管栽培灌溉，勿作枝想，勿作叶想，勿作花想，勿作实想。悬想何益，但不忘栽培之功，怕没有枝叶花实？[①]

---

① 王守仁. 传习录译注 [M]. 王晓昕, 译注. 北京：中华书局, 2018: 70.

本讲练习

1. 积极心理学之父马丁·塞利格曼（Martin Seligman）于2002年提出了幸福的1.0理论（Authentic happiness theory）。在之后的十年中，他吸纳别人的批评意见，不断地发展、完善自己的理论，并于十年后年提出了幸福的2.0理论（Well-being theory）。Happiness在新的理论中为何被Well-being一词取代了呢？在下面两个选段中，塞林格曼讲述了幸福1.0理论到幸福2.0理论的转变。请仔细阅读下面两个选段，判断该选段可能的出处和目标读者。

选段一

The theory in *Authentic Happiness* is that happiness could be analyzed into three different elements that we choose for their own sakes: positive emotion, engagement, and meaning. And each of these elements is better defined and more measurable than happiness. The first is positive emotion; what we feel: pleasure, rapture, ecstasy, warmth, comfort, and the like. An entire life led successfully around this element, I call the "pleasant life."

The second element, engagement, is about flow: being one with the music, time stopping, and the loss of self-consciousness during an absorbing activity. I refer to a life lived with these aims as the "engaged life." Engagement is different, even opposite, from positive emotion; for if you ask people who are in flow what they are thinking and feeling, they usually say, "nothing." In flow we merge with the object. I believe that the concentrated attention that flow requires uses up all the cognitive and emotional resources that make up thought and feeling.

......

There is yet a third element of happiness, which is meaning. I go into flow playing bridge, but after a long tournament, when I look in the mirror, I worry that I am merely fidgeting until I die. The pursuit of engagement and the pursuit of pleasure are often solitary, solipsistic endeavors. Human beings, ineluctably, want meaning and purpose in life. The Meaningful Life consists in belonging to and serving something that you believe is bigger than the self, and humanity creates all the positive institutions to allow this: religion, political party, being green, the Boy Scouts, or the family.

......

Well-being is a construct, and happiness is a thing. A "real thing" is a directly measurable entity. Such an entity can be "operationalized"—which means that a highly specific set of measures defines it. For instance, the windchill factor in meteorology is defined by the combination of temperature and wind at which water freezes (and frost-bite occurs). Authentic happiness theory is an attempt to explain a real thing—happiness—as defined by life satisfaction, where on a 1-to-10 ladder, people rate their satisfaction with their lives. People who have the most positive emotion, the most engagement, and the most meaning in life are the happiest, and they have the most life satisfaction. Well-being theory denies that the topic of positive psychology is a real thing; rather the topic is a construct—well-being—which in turn has several measurable elements, each a real thing, each contributing to well-being, but none defining well-being.

In meteorology, "weather" is such a construct. Weather is not in and of itself a real thing. Several elements, each operationalizable and thus each a real thing, contribute to the weather: temperature, humidity, wind speed, barometric pressure, and the like. Imagine that our topic were not the study of positive psychology but the study of "freedom." How would we go about studying freedom scientifically? Freedom is a construct, not a real thing, and several different elements contribute to it: how free the citizens feel, how often the press is censored, the frequency of elections, the ratio of representatives to population, how many officials are corrupt, among other factors. Each of these elements, unlike the construct of freedom itself, is a measurable thing, but only by measuring these elements do we get an overall picture of how much freedom there is.

Well-being is just like "weather" and "freedom" in its structure: no single measure defines it exhaustively (in jargon, "defines exhaustively" is called "operationalizes"), but several things contribute to it; these are the elements of well-being, and each of the elements is a measurable thing. By contrast, life satisfaction operationalizes happiness in authentic happiness theory just as temperature and wind speed define windchill. Importantly, the elements of well-being are themselves different kinds of things; they are not all mere self-reports of thoughts and feelings of positive emotion, of how engaged you are, and of how much meaning you have in life, as in the original theory of authentic happiness. So the construct of well-being, not the entity of life satisfaction, is the focal topic of positive psychology. Enumerating the elements of well-being is our next task.

这个段落可能的出处是_____，目标读者是_____。

选段二

According to Seligman (2011), the notion of "happiness" is an unwieldy construct that hides the true multifaceted nature of human flourishing. Happiness may constitute the overarching goal of positive psychology, but it does not play any part in a valid and useful theory of human wellbeing. In the first version of his theory, Seligman (2002) claimed that "happiness" was composed of three subjective facets: positive emotion, engagement, and meaning. Happiness was therefore achievable by pursuing one or more of these facets. As a result, individuals low in one aspect could still be "happy" if they nurtured other components. Individuals low in positive emotions could, for instance, flourish by being highly engaged in their lives, or by cultivating a rich sense of meaning.

Seligman (2011) recently revised his original theory by adding two facets to his original account: positive relationships and accomplishment. In addition, Seligman redefined the endpoint of his theory as "well-being" rather than "happiness" in order to stress the multifaceted nature of human flourishing, and to prevent the usual confusion that is often made between "happiness" and "cheerfulness." Seligman's new theory therefore posits that wellbeing consists of the nurturing of one or more of the five following elements: Positive emotion, Engagement, Relationships, Meaning, and Accomplishment (abbreviated as the acronym PERMA). These five elements are the best approximation of what humans pursue *for their own sake,* which is why they have a place in Well-being Theory. Although individuals may sometimes pursue these elements for other ends (e.g., they may for instance think that accomplishment will bring positive emotion), many choose to do so because these elements are intrinsically motivating by themselves.

Seligman's theory also reconciles differing perspectives on the theory and measurement of wellbeing by including both hedonic and eudaimonic aspects of wellbeing, and by allowing for (and encouraging) the measurement of each element using both objective and subjective approaches. Such measures are currently being developed. In addition, measurements of PERMA need to examine how the various facets of wellbeing need to be weighted if researchers or policy-makers want to be able to come up with a single summary measure.

这个段落可能的出处是_____，目标读者是_____。

2. 马丁·塞利格曼和他的研究团队设计了 5 个幸福练习，比较了 5 个幸福练习对于个体幸福感提升和抑郁症改善的情况。下面的两个选段都介绍了这项实验。选段一①于 2005 年发表在学术期刊《美国心理学家》上；选段二②于 2011 年发表在专著《持续的幸福》上。请从内容和语言（时间词、意图性/原因性小句、人称代词、语态、选词）两个方面比较选段一与选段二的异同。

选段一

Internet-Based Interventions

We used the Internet to recruit participants, to deliver the intervention, and to collect our data (Prochaska, Di-Clemente, Velicer, & Rossi, 1993). At this stage in our intervention research, this convenience sample served our purposes well, because on average we have 300 new registrants every day to our Web site (www.authentichappiness.org), which contains many of the positive questionnaires for free. But we also believe that this sample may be at least equal to, and perhaps superior to, college sophomores or clinic volunteers in its scientific

---

① SELIGMAN M, STEEN T, PARK N, PETERSON C. Positive psychology progress: Empirical validation of interventions [J]. American Psychologist, 2005, 60 (5): 410−421.

② SELIGMAN M. Flourish: A visionary new understanding of happiness and well-being [M]. New York: Simon & Schuster, 2011.

justification. One small advantage of collecting data via the Internet is that it obviates data entry by the researcher (and associated human error). One larger advantage is substantial cost-effectiveness in large-sample studies. After one pays for Web site development and maintenance, there are virtually no additional costs to data collection for adequately powered studies, and we have offered the use of our Web site to interested researchers.

Much more scientifically important, and controversial, is the possibility of biased sampling. Gosling, Vazire, Srivastava, and John (2004) compared survey data collected via the Internet with survey data collected via traditional methods. They concluded that (a) Internet data are just as diverse as data collected via traditional methods, (b) participants who voluntarily participate in Web-based studies are no more psychologically disturbed than traditional participants, and (c) participants in Internet studies are no less likely to take the study seriously or to provide accurate information than are participants in traditional samples. We believe our sample is biased but in a relevant direction. It is tilted toward those who want to become happier, precisely those who are the ultimate target of our interventions. We would not want to generalize our findings to people who do not want to become happier or to people who have to be coerced into taking psychological tests. On the basis of these considerations, we chose to use the Internet.

Procedure

For our first large RCT, we designed five happiness exercises and one placebo control exercise. Each exercise was delivered via the Internet and could be completed within one week. One of these exercises focused on building gratitude, two focused on increasing awareness of what is most positive about oneself, and two focused on identifying strengths of character. In a randomized, placebo-controlled study, we compared the effects of these exercises with those of what we thought would be a plausible placebo control: journaling for one week about early memories. We followed our participants for six months, periodically measuring symptoms of both depression and happiness.

We recruited a convenience sample from among visitors to the Web site created for Seligman's (2002) book *Authentic Happiness* by creating a link called "Happiness Exercises." The study was described on the site as an opportunity to help test new exercises designed to increase happiness. Over the course of approximately one month, we recruited 577 adult participants,

42% male and 58% female. Almost two thirds of the participants (64%) were between the ages of 35 and 54 years. Of the participants surveyed, 39% had a degree from a four-year college, and 27% had some graduate school education. Notably, only 4% of the participants did not have education or vocational training after high school, another limit on the generalizability of our findings. Consistent with their reported levels of education, approximately three fourths of the participants classified their income levels as "average" or above. The sample was largely White (77%).

Visitors to the site were told that the exercise they were to receive was not guaranteed to make them happier and that they might receive an inert (placebo) exercise. We did not offer any initial financial incentives for doing the exercises. In order to ensure good follow-up, we did tell participants, however, that upon completion of follow-up tests at one week, one month, three months, and six months after completing the exercise, they would be entered into a lottery. The lottery prizes included one $500 award and three $100 awards.

After participants agreed to the terms presented, they answered a series of basic demographic questions and completed two questionnaires, the SHI and the CES-D, as already described.

Then participants received a randomly assigned exercise. Participants were encouraged to print out or write down the instructions for their exercise and to keep them accessible during the week to come. They were instructed to return to the Web site to complete follow-up questionnaires after completing their assigned exercise.

Participants received reminder e-mails. The first reminder, sent early in the week, repeated the instructions for their assigned exercise. They were also given contact information and encouraged to contact the researchers with any questions or concerns. The second reminder e-mail, sent later in the week, reminded participants to return to the Web site for the follow-up questionnaires: "Thank you again for participating in our study. Please remember to return to [url] by [relevant date] to give us feedback about your exercise and to complete follow-up questionnaires."

When participants returned to the Web site after performing their exercise, they completed the same measures of happiness and depression administered at pretest. In addition, participants answered a manipulation check question to assess whether they had in fact completed the exercise as instructed during the relevant time period (scored *yes* or *no*).

Of the 577 participants who completed baseline questionnaires, 411 (71%) completed all five follow-up assessments. Participants who dropped out of the study did not differ from those who remained on their baseline happiness or depression scores, nor was there differential dropout from the six exercises. We include in our analyses only those participants who completed all follow-up questionnaires.

Detailed descriptions of the exercises are available from us upon request. However, the following paragraphs present overviews of each:

Placebo control exercise: Early memories. Participants were asked to write about their early memories every night for one week.

Gratitude visit. Participants were given one week to write and then deliver a letter of gratitude in person to someone who had been especially kind to them but had never been properly thanked.

Three good things in life. Participants were asked to write down three things that went well each day and their causes every night for one week. In addition, they were asked to provide a causal explanation for each good thing.

You at your best. Participants were asked to write about a time when they were at their best and then to reflect on the personal strengths displayed in the story. They were told to review their story once every day for a week and to reflect on the strengths they had identified.

Using signature strengths in a new way. Participants were asked to take our inventory of character strengths online at www.authentichappiness.org and to receive individualized feedback about their top five ("signature") strengths (Peterson et al., 2005a). They were then asked to use one of these top strengths in a new and different way every day for one week.

Identifying signature strengths. This exercise was a truncated version of the one just described, without the instruction to use signature strengths in new ways. Participants were asked to take the survey, to note their five highest strengths, and to use them more often during the next week.

选段二

Here's a brief exercise that will raise your well-being and lower your depression:

The Gratitude Visit

Close your eyes. Call up the face of someone still alive who years ago did something or said something that changed your life for the better. Someone who you never properly thanked; someone you could meet face-to-face next week. Got a face?

Gratitude can make your life happier and more satisfying. When we feel gratitude, we benefit from the pleasant memory of a positive event in our life. Also, when we express our gratitude to others, we strengthen our relationship with them. But sometimes our thank-you is said so casually or quickly that it is nearly meaningless. In this exercise, called the "Gratitude Visit," you will have the opportunity to experience what it is like to express your gratitude in a thoughtful, purposeful manner.

Your task is to write a letter of gratitude to this individual and deliver it in person. The letter should be concrete and about three hundred words: be specific about what she did for you and how it affected your life. Let her know what you are doing now, and mention how you often remember what she did. Make it sing!

Once you have written the testimonial, call the person and tell her you'd like to visit her, but be vague about the purpose of the meeting; this exercise is much more fun when it is a surprise. When you meet her, take your time reading your letter. Notice her reactions as well as yours. If she interrupts you as you read, say that you really want her to listen until you are done. After you have read the letter (every word), discuss the content and your feelings for each other.

You will be happier and less depressed one month from now.

…

Here's a second exercise to give you the flavor of the interventions that we have validated in random-assignment, placebo-controlled designs:

What-Went-Well Exercise (Also Called "Three Blessings")

Every night for the next week, set aside ten minutes before you go to sleep. Write down three things that went well today and why they went well. You may use a journal or your computer to write about the events, but it is important that you have a physical record of what you wrote. The three things need not be earthshaking in importance ("My husband picked up my favorite ice cream for dessert on the way home from work today"), but they can be important ("My sister just gave birth to a healthy baby boy").

Next to each positive event, answer the question "Why did this happen?" For example, if you wrote that your husband picked up ice cream, write "because my husband is really thoughtful sometimes" or "because I remembered to call him from work and remind him to stop by the grocery store." Or if you wrote, "My sister just gave birth to a healthy baby boy," you might pick as the cause "God was looking out for her" or "She did everything right during her pregnancy."

Writing about why the positive events in your life happened may seem awkward at first, but please stick with it for one week. It will get easier. The odds are that you will be less depressed, happier, and addicted to this exercise six months from now.

...

Let me first tell you about why I constructed the website,

which has all the major validated tests of the positive side of life, with feedback on where you stand. This website is free and is intended as a public service. It is also a gold mine for positive psychology researchers, much better for obtaining valid results than asking questions, as researchers usually do, of college sophomores or clinic volunteers.

At this writing 1.8 million people have registered at the website and taken the tests. Between 500 and 1,500 new people register every day, and every so often I put up a link. One link is about exercises. People who go to this link are invited to help us test new exercises. First they take depression and happiness tests, such as the Center for Epidemiological Studies depression scale and the authentic happiness inventory, which are both on www.authentichappiness.org. Next we randomly assign them to a single exercise that is either active or a placebo. All exercises require two to three hours over the course of one week. In our first web study, we tried six exercises, including the gratitude visit and what-went-well.

Of the 577 participants who completed the baseline questionnaires, 471 completed all five follow-up assessments. We found that participants in all conditions (including the placebo-control condition, which was to write up a childhood memory every night for a week) were happier and less depressed one week after they received their assigned exercise. Thereafter, people in the control condition were no happier or less depressed than they were at baseline.

Two of the exercises—what-went-well and the signature strengths exercise below—markedly lowered depression three months and six months later. These two exercises also substantially increased happiness through six months. The gratitude visit produced large decreases in depression and large increases in happiness one month later, but the effect faded three months later. Not surprisingly, we found that the degree to which participants actively continue their assigned exercise beyond the prescribed one-week period predicted how long the changes in happiness last.

Signature Strengths Exercise

The purpose of this exercise is to encourage you to own your signature strengths by finding new and more frequent uses for them. A signature strength has the following hallmarks:

- sense of ownership and authenticity ("This is the real me")

- feeling of excitement while displaying it, particularly at first
- rapid learning curve as the strength is first practiced
- sense of yearning to find new ways to use it
- feeling of inevitability in using the strength ("Try to stop me")
- Invigoration rather than exhaustion while using the strength
- The creation and pursuit of personal projects that revolve around it
- Joy, zest, enthusiasm, even ecstasy while using it

Now please take the strengths survey. If you do not have access to the web, you can go to the Appendix and take a brief version of this test. On the website, you will get your results immediately and can print them out if you like. This questionnaire was developed by Chris Peterson, a professor at the University of Michigan, and has been taken by more than a million people from two hundred nations. You will have the benefit of being able to compare yourself to other people like you.

As you complete the questionnaire, pay most attention to the rank order of your own strengths. Were there any surprises for you? Next, take your five highest strengths one at a time and ask yourself, "Is it a signature strength?"

After you have completed the test, perform the following exercise: this week I want you to create a designated time in your schedule when you will exercise one or more of your signature strengths in a new way either at work or at home or in leisure—just make sure that you create a clearly defined opportunity to use it. For example:

- If your signature strength is creativity, you may choose to set aside two hours one evening to begin working on a screenplay.
- If you identify hope/optimism as a strength, you might write a column for the local newspaper in which you express hope about the future of the space program.
- If you claim self-control as a strength, you might choose to work out at the gym rather than watch TV one evening.
- If your strength is an appreciation of beauty and excellence, you might take a longer, more beautiful route to and from work, even though it adds twenty minutes more to your commute.

> The best thing to do is to create the new way of using your strength yourself. Write about your experience. How did you feel before, during, and after engaging in the activity? Was the activity challenging? Easy? Did time pass quickly? Did you lose your sense of self-consciousness? Do you plan to repeat the exercise?
>
> These positive psychology exercises worked on me, they worked on my family, they worked on my students, and they were taught to professionals and then worked on their clients—even very depressed clients. And the exercises even worked in the gold-standard testing of placebo-controlled, random assignment.

3. 请从自己的专业领域找出同一作者（或研究团队）针对同一话题撰写的、出处不同的两个段落。试着从目标读者的角度分析两个段落的异同。

第二讲　论　证

学术写作不强调修辞和文采，强调的是论证。论证是逻辑学上的一个重要概念。当我们说一篇学术文章"有逻辑""没逻辑"的时候，说的就是论证。

这一讲，我们谈谈学术写作中的论证（argument）①。论证，简单地说，**就是拿出一组前提（premises）支持一个结论（conclusion）的推理过程**。

叶圣陶先生在《怎样写作》中说：

> 我们可以设一个譬喻，要把材料组成一个圆球，才算到了完成的地步。圆球这东西最是美满，浑凝调和，周遍一致，恰是一篇独立的、有生命的文字的象征。圆球有一个中心，各部分都向中心环拱着。而各部分又必密合无间，不容更动，方得成为圆球。一篇文字的各部分也应环拱于中心（这是指所要写出的总旨，如对于一件事情的论断，蕴蓄于中而非吐

---

① 并非所有类型的学术写作都需要论证，但如果我们想通过学术写作觉悟未知、促发新知，便一定会涉及论证了。

不可的情感之类），为着中心而存在。[①]

　　这段话虽非针对学术写作而言，但对学术写作的启示颇多。圆球的"中心"就是论证的"结论"，"各部分"就是"一组前提"，"向中心环拱"就是我们使用"一组前提"支持"结论"的推理过程。

　　不同学科的学术研究遵循着非常相似的论证逻辑：我们希望通过一番科学论证，得出一个"真"的结论。科学论证最常见的三种方式是演绎论证、归纳论证和类比论证。演绎论证是由一般原理推导出关于个别情况的结论；归纳论证是由具体的事例推导出关于一般原理、原则的结论；类比论证是借由事物之间的相似性，从个别情况出发，推导出关于个别情况的结论。我们下面分别看看如何在三类论证中得到"真"的结论。

　　先看演绎论证。如何在演绎论证中得到一个"真"的结论呢？我们需要理解演绎论证里两个非常重要的概念。一是论证的有效性（validity），二是论证的可靠性（soundness）。

　　什么是论证的有效性呢？简单地说，如果前提为真，那么结论必然为真的论证具有论证的有效性。根据这个定义，看看下面两个论证哪一个具有有效性。

论证 1：	论证 2：
所有 A 都是 B。（前提）	所有 A 都是 B。（前提）
C 是 A。（前提）	C 是 B。（前提）
因此，C 是 B。（结论）	因此，C 是 A。（结论）

[①] 叶圣陶. 怎样写作［M］. 北京：中华书局，2007: 13.

同学们不难发现：在论证 1 中，前提如果为真，结论不可能为假。比如在"所有金属都能导电。铜是金属。铜能导电"这个论证中，结论能从前提中必然得出，前提蕴含着结论。然而，论证 2 中，即便前提为真，也不能保证结论为真。比如在"所有金属都能导电。铜能导电。因此，铜是金属"这个论证中，结论为真；但在"所有金属都能导电。石墨能导电。因此，石墨是金属"这个论证中，结论为假。于是我们得出，论证 1 是一个有效的论证形式，基于有效论证形式做出的论证是有效论证。

演绎论证的有效性和前提、结论事实上的真假无关。换言之，演绎论证的有效性只和前提和结论的逻辑关系有关。在下面这个演绎论证中，虽然前提和结论事实上都为假，但这个演绎论证依然是一个有效的论证。

所有猪都会飞。（前提 1）
所有会飞的事物都会游泳。（前提 2）
所以，所有的猪都会游泳。（结论）

下面，我们再来看看什么是演绎论证的可靠性。由于有效的演绎论证里可能会包含着错误的结论，我们不能只看到一个演绎论证逻辑上有效，就草率地接受了该论证中的结论。我们需要进一步审视是否所有的前提都为真。如果一个演绎论证是有效的，并且所有的前提都为真，我们说这样的演绎论证是可靠的。

下面我们通过一个例子来看看如何将有效论证上升为可靠

论证。

　　2022年初的北京冬奥会上,中国选手任子威获得男子1000米短道速滑金牌。比赛中,任子威并不是物理意义上第一个冲过终点的,但裁判员反复观看回放录像后,认定第一个冲过终点的匈牙利选手应被取消比赛名次。短短的几分钟里,裁判员完成了"匈牙利选手应被取消比赛名次"的论证。论证过程如下:

　　　　所有犯规的选手应被取消比赛名次。(前提1)
　　　　匈牙利选手犯规了。(前提2)
　　　　匈牙利选手应被取消比赛名次。(结论)[1]

　　其中,"所有犯规的选手应被取消比赛名次"是前提1,"匈牙利选手犯规了"是前提2,"匈牙利选手应被取消比赛名次"是结论。如果此论证中的两个前提都成立,那么结论必然成立。
　　那么这个逻辑上有效的论证是不是一个可靠的论证呢?将逻辑上有效的论证上升为可靠论证的关键在于前提为真。对于这个论证来讲,"所有犯规的选手应被取消比赛名次"是短道速滑比赛中几乎尽人皆知的规则,不太需要论证;而"匈牙利选手犯规了"是这个论证成为可靠论证的关键。换言之,前提2并非不言自明,需要充分论证。那么,裁判是如何得出"匈牙利选手犯规了"这个结论的呢?

---

[1]　这个论证可抽象为:因为所有的A都是B,且C是A。所以C是B。

如果选手在比赛中有下列情形之一：（1）脱轨（Off-track）；（2）阻挡（Impeding）；（3）协助犯规（Assistance）；（4）蹬踢冰刀（Kicking out），则选手将被判犯规。（前提1）

匈牙利选手有阻挡行为。（前提2）

匈牙利选手犯规了。（结论）

可见，在裁定匈牙利选手犯规时，裁判员实际上又完成了一次论证①。同上，我们要确定这个逻辑有效的论证是可靠论证，就得确保大前提和小前提为真。参照国际滑联的最新规则②，不难得出大前提为真；而小前提是否真，则需要进一步的论证。那么，裁判是如何认定"匈牙利选手有阻挡行为"的呢？根据国际滑联官网，通过比赛现场录像的回放，对匈牙利选手阻挡犯规的认定如下：

Hungarian Skater LIU Shaolin Sandor was making a pass on the straight but did not manage to level on time with REN Ziwei (CHN), therefore he did not have the priority to enter the corner. For the second penalty for LIU Shaolin Sandor, the Chief Referee pointed out that this penalty was for an arm block at the finish, the

---

① 这个论证可抽象为：如果A，那么B。A。因此B。

② International Skating Union. Special regulations and technical rules: Short tracking speeding skating [EB/OL]. (2022-09-13) [2022-11-01]. https://isu.org/inside-isu/rules-regulations/isu-statutes-constitution-regulations-technical/special-regulations-and-technical-rules/29385-short-track-speed-skating-2022/file

arm block happened twice and therefore had to be called.①

可见，匈牙利选手的第一次阻挡发生在直道进入弯道时，由于其在直道滑行的位置是在蓝线内，不具备进入弯道的优先权，强行超越、造成阻挡（见图2-1）；第二次阻挡发生在临近终点处。匈牙利选手从弯道又进入直道后，两次用手臂阻挡了内道选手的滑行（见图2-2）②。至此，大、小前提都为真，我们可以放心地认为"匈牙利选手犯规了"这个结论为真。

图2-1　　　　　　　　　图2-2

再来看归纳论证。如何在归纳论证中得到一个"真"的结论呢？在刚才的论证中，我们从裁判的视角，经演绎论证得出"匈牙利选手应被取消比赛名次"的结论。作为普通观众，我们可能不懂得那么多的比赛规则，不过若是一场比赛接一场比赛地看下

---

① International Skating Union. ISU statement: Short track speed skating men 1000m competition at Beijing 2022 Olympic Winter Games ［EB/OL］. (2022-02-07) ［2022-11-01］. https://www.isu.org/isu-news/news/145-news/13972-isu-statement-isu-short-track-speed-skating-men-1000m-competition? templateParam=15

② International Skating Union. ISU E-learning ［EB/OL］.［2022-11-01］. https://elearning.isu.org/login/index.php

来，不难在头脑中构建出如下论证。

前提 1：强行超越的韩国选手×××被判犯规了。
前提 2：强行超越的匈牙利选手×××被判犯规了。
……
前提 n：强行超越的×××选手被判犯规了。
结论：选手若在比赛中强行超越会被判犯规。

　　经如此归纳论证得出的结论是否为"真"呢？归纳论证若想得到必然为真的结论，除了保证前提为真，也要保证考察了所有前提中个体的情况，无一遗漏。事实上，完全归纳论证是极少的。我们通常只能基于整体中一些典型个案的情况，做不完全的归纳论证。在不完全归纳论证中，我们无法得到必然为"真"的结论。

　　由于无法得到必然为"真"的结论，在归纳论证中，我们不用"有效性""可靠性"，而用"力度""可接受度"评价归纳论证的质量。在一个有力度、可接受度高的归纳论证中，如果前提为真，结论极有可能为真。比如你此时正在看北京冬奥会最后一场短道速滑比赛。如果之前的所有比赛中，强行超越的选手都被判犯规了，那我们可以断定在最后这一场比赛中，强行超越选手被判犯规的可能性是极大的，也就是我们的结论极有可能为真。

　　以上我们以一个生活中的例子展示了学术研究中最常见的两种论证逻辑。科学研究中的论证和例子中的论证本质上相同，不过我们往往需要通过实验设计及亲自收取、分析的数据论证某个前提为真。落实在写作上，这个部分构成了文章的核心。牛顿曾对自然科学研究中归纳和演绎的论证逻辑做了很好的总结：

> 在自然哲学里，像在数学里一样，用分析方法研究困难的事物，应当总是先于综合的方法。这种分析包括做实验和观察，用归纳法去从中引出普遍结论，并且使这些结论没有异议的余地，除非这些异议是从实验或者其他肯定的事实得出的。因为在实验哲学中是不考虑什么假说的。尽管用归纳法从实验和观察中进行论证不是普遍的结论的证明，可是它是事物的本性所许可的最好的论证方法，并且随着归纳的愈普遍，这种论证看来也愈为有力。如果在现象中没有出现例外，那么结论就可声称是普遍的。但是如果以后在任何时候从实验中出现了例外，那么就可以开始声称有这样的例外存在……这就是分析的方法；而综合的方法则假定原因已找到，并且已确立为原理，再用这些原理去解释由它们发生的现象，并证明这些解释。①

最后我们说一下类比论证。由于类比论证是基于事物的相似性推断一个事物的特质也存在于另一个事物上，评估这类论证的关键就在于：（1）判断这种相似性是否真实存在；（2）判断某种特质是不是真实地存在于某个事物上。

---

① 牛顿. 牛顿光学（第二版）[M]. 周岳明，舒幼生，邢峰，熊汉富，译. 北京：北京大学出版社，2011: 258-259.

科学家基于对生活的观察和事物之间相似性的察觉提出了很多伟大的科学假设。比如，奥地利医生奥恩伯格受到父亲叩击酒桶便能得知酒桶里酒的存量的启发，提出了"叩诊法"，用以诊断病人中胸腔中积水的情况。再如，自人类1903年发明飞机以来，科学家一直被飞机飞行两翼有害的"颤振"现象困扰。飞行设计师注意到蜻蜓翅膀前缘上方的"翅痣"并发现：如果把这块黑痣切除后再放飞，蜻蜓就会荡来荡去，无法保持平稳飞行。于是他们提出大胆的科学设想：如果在飞机机翼末段的前缘安装一块类似"翅痣"的加厚区，可以消除颤振现象。

可见类比推理是一些科学研究的起点，也有一些科学研究的主要结论就是通过类比论证得出的。在一篇著名的论文《为堕胎辩护》[1]中，哲学家朱迪斯·汤普森（Judith Thomson）认为堕胎是合理的。他为我们勾勒了一个情境：假设你醒来时发现自己和一名已失去意识的著名小提琴家同床共枕。这个小提琴家患有致命的肾脏疾病，某音乐社团的人发现只有你能够为其提供血液配型。这些音乐发烧友绑架了你，并将他体内的循环系统移到了你的身上。你的肾脏可以排除他体内的毒素，与他分离意味着杀死他。而你若能坚持九个月，他会痊愈。现在的问题是：你是否有拯救小提琴家的义务呢？作者的论证逻辑是：面对生病的音乐家和面对腹中胎儿的情境是可比的，我们没有将血液系统分享给小提琴家的义务；同样的，一个孕妇也没有将循环系统分享给胎儿的义务。

---

[1] THOMSON J J. A defense of abortion [G]// HUMBER J M, ALMEDER R F, Biomedical ethics and the law. MA, Boston: Springer, 1971: 266-273.

这一类比论证的结论可靠吗？作者的结论是否说服了你？你能否从评估类比论证的两个方面思考一下呢？我把这个问题留给大家思考。

无论遵从上述哪一种论证逻辑，好的论证除了给出自己一方的前提和结论，通常也能考虑到与自身相异的论证。同学们经常有的一个困惑是，引入和自身相异的论证，会不会削弱作者的声音？在我看来，考虑到自身观点的反面，不仅不会削弱作者的声音，反而有机会增强论证的力量，凸显作者的见解。我们举两个例子加以说明。

先来看一个人文社科的例子。这个例子来自屠龙为明代高濂《遵生八笺》①一书写的序中。屠龙以"人生实难，有生必灭"开篇，列举若干"现代人"的通病，即"精耗于嗜欲，身疲于过劳，

---

① 屠龙. 屠龙序 [M] //高濂. 遵生八笺. 杭州：浙江古籍出版社，2017: 1.

心烦于营求,智昏于思虑。身坐几席而神驰八荒,数在刹那而计营万祀,揽其所必不任,觊其所必不可得",说明"生有可遵之理"。

然后,作者用几个总体原则和一系列精彩的比喻论述当如何"遵生",即"知滔淫之荡精,故绝嗜寡欲以处清静;知沉思之耗气,故戒思少虑以宅恬愉;知疲劳之损形,故节慎起居以宁四大;知贪求之败德,故抑远外物以甘萧寥。畏侵耗如利刃,避伤损如寇仇,护元和如婴儿,宝灵明如拱璧,防漏败如航海,严出入如围城",并介绍了《遵生八笺》作者高濂在"遵生"方面的实践。

文章若到此结束,似乎也没什么问题。但作者却话锋一转,以"或谓"为始,站在"反对者"的立场,提出不同意此般遵生的观点。

> 或谓大道以虚无为宗,有身以染著为累,今观高子所叙,居室运用,游具品物,宝玩古器,书画香草花木之类,颇极烦冗。研而讨之,驰扰神思;聚而蓄之,障阂身心,其于本来虚空,了无一法之旨,亦甚戾矣,何遵生之为?

最后,作者就"反对者"的观点,鲜明地指出"余曰不然",并陈述了自己的理由,驳斥了相左的观点。

> 余曰不然,人心之体,本来虚空,奈何物态纷拏,汩没已久,一旦欲扫而空之,无所栖泊。及至驰骤漂荡而不知止,一切药物补元,器玩娱志,心有所寄,庶不外驰,亦清净之本也。

中国古代虽没有"论文"的概念，但这篇文章实在"论"得精彩！尽可能考虑不同的观点、立场和角度，会让我们自身持有的观点更为读者信服。

我们再来看一个自然科学的例子——在科学史上持续三百年的"波粒之争"。自17世纪始，科学家开始研究光的本质。关于光的本质，有两种假说：一个是以惠更斯为代表的"波动说"，一个是以牛顿为代表的"微粒说"。下面是惠更斯《光论》[1]和牛顿《光学》[2]中的两段节选。

惠更斯《光论》

（第五章，第21节）

依照我先前的建立的理论，这种双折射似乎需要光波的一种双重辐射，两种波都是球面的，只是其中一束波比另一束行进得慢些。因此，正如我在冰洲石情形下所作的那样，只要假定物质是传播这些波的媒介，就十分容易解释这种现象。这样，承认在同一物体中有波的两种辐射就没什么麻烦了。**由于可能曾经有人反对**，在组成由具有确定外形和规则堆积的相同微粒的两种晶体时，微粒留下的充满"以太"物质的空隙不足以去传递我们在那里给定的光波，我假定这些微粒

---

[1] 惠更斯. 光论［M］. 蔡勖，译. 北京：北京大学出版社，2012：54.
[2] 牛顿. 牛顿光学（第二版）［M］. 周岳明，舒幼生，邢峰，熊汉富，译. 北京：北京大学出版社，2011：235.

具有一种罕见的构造,更恰当地说,假定它们由其他更小的微粒所组成,"以太"物质可以自由地在它们之间穿过,从而排除了这一困难。此外,从有关物体是由更小的物质组成的论证,也必定得到这一点。

牛顿《光学》

(疑问28,第3段)

到目前为止还只有(就我所知)惠更斯一人试图用压力或运动的传播来说说冰洲石晶体中的反常折射,为此目的他假设在这种晶体中有两种不同的振动媒质。但是当他在两块相继的该晶体中试验这些折射现象,并发现了他们具有前面所提到的那些情况时;他承认自己不知如何来解释它们。因为从一个发光物体通过一个均匀媒质传播出去的压力或运动,必须在所有方面上都一样;然而根据那些实验,看来光线在它们的不同方面上有着不同的性质。他推测,通过第一块晶体的以太脉动会受到某些新的变异,这种新的变异可能使这些以太脉动在第二块晶体内随着该晶体的位置而决定在这一种或那一种媒质中传播。但是那些变异是什么,他说不出来,也想不出满足这一点的任何东西。而且如果他已经知道这种反常折射并不依赖于新的变异,而是依赖于光线的原有的并且使不变的属性,那么要揭示那些他认为是由第一块

> 晶体加于光线上的属性怎么又会在入射到该晶体之前就已存在于光线中,以及一般地说,由发光物体发射的一切光线怎么会一开始就具有这些属性,他会感到困难。至少对我来说,如果光仅仅是在以太中传播的压力或运动,那么这似乎也是解释不通的。

从以上两个选段,我们也可以感受到两位科学家不同的论证风格。相较而言,惠更斯更加温和,并没有指出反对者是谁("由于可能曾经有人反对"的英文原文是"since it might have been objected that…"),显示出一种"对事不对人"的论证风格;牛顿似乎没有惠更斯含蓄和委婉,"他承认自己不知"("he confessed himself at a loss"),"……他说不出来,也想不出……"("…he could not say, nor think of anything satisfactory…"),"如果他已经知道,……他会感到困难"("And if he had known that, … he would have found it as difficult…"),可见牛顿更犀利、针锋相对的论证风格。

以上两个例子说明,无论在人文社科还是自然科学领域,完整充分的论证都离不开观点的比较。潘罗斯和盖斯勒认为,和新手作者相比,有经验的写作者更能认识到:

> Texts are authored.
> Authors present knowledge in the form of claims.

> Knowledge claims can conflict.
>
> Knowledge claims can be tested.[1]

一言以蔽之，有经验的写作者更清楚学术写作不仅仅是知识的呈现，更是知识的建构。当我们自信地呈现与他人相异的观点，也是在清楚有力地告诉读者：在考虑了不同视角、不同方案、不同阐释后，这是我当下的观点，我为它负责，希望它能同那些和它相异，甚至对立的观点一起，加入学术共同体的对话中，共同地建构本学科的知识。

论证是学术写作的灵魂。有人说：写一篇好的学术论文，就是讲了一个好的研究故事。我不太认同这个类比。论文中写清楚"在某个背景下，用了某一方法，做了某个实验，获得了某些结果"只是表层，真正赋予学术论文生命力的是论证，是得出可靠的、有力度的结论之前推理的过程。

本讲文末附了我写过的一篇小文：小词不小。看过之后，你不妨思考，看看能不能再举出像 although 这样有神奇论证力量的小词。

---

[1] PENROSE A, GEISLER C. Reading and writing without authority [J]. College Composition and Communication, 1994, 45(4): 505-520.

附：

小词不小

"although"是学术英语里一个极为平凡的小词，小到在各式各样的学术词表里遍寻不着。如果问学生：你喜欢 although 这个词吗？我猜，大部分的学生会答：说不上喜不喜欢，反正它不能与 but 连用就对了。也许少部分的学生会答：它后面得加从句，而不是短词。说不定也会有一两学生能熟练地背出海伦·凯勒的励志名句：

Although the world is full of suffering, it is also full of the overcoming of it.

although 在我心里，大概占据学术词汇 No. 1 的地位。

第一次注意到学术写作中 although 一词，是在 2014 年发表于《第二语言写作杂志》（*Journal of Second Language Writing*）的一篇论文中。我忘记了当时在琢磨什么，总之琢磨的结果是发现有大约 10 个句子是以 although/though 开头的。再次和 although 发生化学反应的催化剂是几年后与外教同事的讨论。这位外教同事来中国工作已很多年，她似乎很早就发现中国学生和学者不擅长用这个词。而最近一次提到 although，是在这学期的学术英语课上，备课那天是端午节，不知道哪来的兴致，我写了一首《我心里面住着两个小精灵》。

Two little elves live in your heart
When one waves
Get started
The other pulls your back
Is it the road less traveled by?
Can you foresee the thorns ahead?

Two little elves live in your heart
When one whispers
Well done
The other turns you down
It isn't that big deal
Only time will tell

Two little elves live in your heart
When one cheers
Come on
The other lends you a shoulder to lean against
Is it worth the years and tears?
Can you put up with the endless toil?

Two little elves live in your heart
Leave neither of them unattended
Till one day you begin a sentence with "although"
You are not simple-minded anymore

"我心里面住着两个小精灵"——诗的每一小节都是以同样的句子开头。我想：学术研究的过程就是心里的两个小精灵共存的过程。一个小精灵说，你的研究有趣、有意义、有价值、值得花时间、值得花力气；而另一个小精灵说，你的研究没趣、没意义、没价值、不值得花时间、不值得花力气。在研究的不同阶段，两个小精灵的声音此消彼长，我们的内心也随之波澜起伏。

我们习惯并觉得舒适的做法是用意念帮着一个小精灵打败另一个小精灵，内心获得安顿之后，在研究报告中呈现稳稳当当的开头（如"在双一流和'一带一路'建设的大背景下"）、稳稳当当的主体（"我研究了什么""我怎么研究的""我得出了什么结论"）以及稳稳当当的结尾（如"本项研究的价值有以下三个方面"）。而我们不太习惯，甚至会引起不适的，是把为什么帮其中的一个小精灵，是怎么打败另一个小精灵的，原原本本地呈现给读者。外教同事和我说，在英文学术写作中，比起回答"是什么"（what），更重要的是回答"为什么"（why）。

当我们给出理论、方法、讨论，比起理论、方法、讨论本身，也许读者更关心的是，为什么在万千解释复杂现象的理论中，选择了某个理论；和众多可行的方法相比，某个方法为何格外适合当下的问题；在若干对结果的解释中，目前这个解释的力度如何。

我们当然可以用 shopping list 的方法去描述这些可能性，但学术语篇要求作者能在有限的文字中精练地传递观点。使用从属连词 although 便是呈现众多可能性的一种非常有效的手段。它明确而有力地向读者表达：经过对不同视角、方案和解释的审视之后，这就是我目前的看法，我对此负责。我希望这一观点能够与那些不同甚至对立的观点一起，参与到学术社区的讨论中，共同构建该学科的知识。

几年前，我写了一篇有关教学的论文，看学生学术写作某一方面的表现，经过了教学干预，有没有获得进步。在这篇论文初稿的方法部分，有这么一句话：

Students were asked to compose a source-based writing after class.

在修改阶段，我集中阅读了不少论文，发现我所在领域的好文章有一个共性：作者不会单纯地描述研究本身，而会想到读者的一些疑问，甚至是质疑，写作中适时地给予回应。例如：

例1：Clearly, both our corpus and the sub-set of editorial statements are quite limited in size. **Nevertheless**, these were all that was available; neither were we able to get an even distribution in the publication dates. Analysing such historical data that is **difficult to come by** as we do in the study can **nevertheless reveal** something about discourse and the social-cultural milieu regarding plagiarism during the historical period in question. （作者在方法部分巧妙地回应了对"数据量偏少"的质疑）

例2：**Although one may say** it is unsurprising that such a practice of blatant copying would be unacceptable in the publishing world of any country at any time, **we believe** its unacceptability and the conceptualisation of the unacceptability is still worth demonstrating in relation to a particular chronotope, as we did in the study reported in this paper. （作者在结论部分巧妙地回应了对"研究价值"的质疑）

后来，我发现这个特点不唯我所在的专业特有，好的学术作者心里似乎都装着一个或多个"异见者"。以下是出现在其他学科学术文章中的一些例子：

例3：…Further adding to the confusion regarding ER flexibility is the widespread agreement that this process—however it is defined—is inherently adaptive. In our view, this assumption is problematic because incorporating the outcome (i.e., adaptiveness) within the conceptualization of a process (i.e., ER flexibility) short-circuits what should be an empirical investigation of the contexts in which such process is (and perhaps is not) helpful.（心理学）

例4：Although it is often assumed in the literature that G is connected and closed, we will not assume closure unless explicitly stated.（数学）

通过对若干类似例子的思考，我逐渐认识到，学术论文的写作应体现对话性。以方法部分为例，我们不仅要回答做了什么，是怎样做的，同时还要展示给作者：这般设计也许存在不足，但不足之处作者在思考与权衡中已充分意识到了。

在修改初稿方法部分的那句话时，我思考了几个问题：是不是会有读者质疑让学生课后完成作文这一设计的合理性？课后完成有哪些缺点？课后完成是不是也有明显的优点？通过怎样的语言表达能够淡化缺点，凸显优点？

经过这一系列的思考，在这篇论文的终稿里，这句话后补充了：

Although out-of-class homework opens itself up to outside assistance (thesaurus, peer editing, etc.), it allows more writing time for the students, lowers their anxiety, and avoids the interruption of the existing curriculum.

although 的使用体现了淡化缺点、凸显优点的需要。相比于初稿，这句话增强了方法部分的论证力量。读者会觉得，研究者在实验的每一步，都经过了细致的考虑，做了谨慎的决定，不仅交代了"是什么"，还回答了"为什么"。同时，对话的空间也打开了：其他研究者完全可以用当堂测试的方法再做实验，比照结果。

可见 although 这个小词不小，它关涉到我们如何看待知识。学术写作终究不仅是为了知识的呈现，更是为了知识的建构。

愿有一日，我和我的学生们，能从容、平和地看待心里的两个小精灵。那时的我们早已不求其中的一个能打败另一个，而是安静地看着她们对话，然后轻盈地站在其中一个的身后。

本讲练习

1. 下面是来自卡尔·刘易斯的小说《爱丽丝梦游仙境》①的一些选段。请判断段落中涉及的论证类型,并判断该论证是不是高质量的论证。

(1) Alice was beginning to get very tired of sitting by her sister on the bank and of having nothing to do: once or twice she had peeped into the book her sister was reading, but it had no pictures or conversations in it, "and what is the use of a book," thought Alice, "without pictures or conversations?"

(2) "Well," thought Alice to herself. "After such a fall as this, I shall think nothing of tumbling downstairs! How brave they'll all think me at home! Why I wouldn't say anything about it, even if I fell off the top of the house!"

(3) Soon her eye fell on a little glass box that was lying under the table: she opened it, and found in it a small cake, on which the words "EAT ME" were beautifully marked in currants. "Well, I'll eat it," said Alice, "and if it makes me grow

---

① CARROLL L. Alice's adventures in wonderland and through the looking-glass [M]. Oxford: Oxford University Press, 2009.

larger, I can reach the key; and if it makes me grow smaller, I can creep under the door: so either way I'll get into the garden, and I don't care which happens."

(4)"Well! What are you?" said the Pigeon. "I can see you're trying to invent something!"

"I—I'm a little girl," said Alice, rather doubtfully, as she remembered the number of changes she had gone through, that day.

"A likely story indeed!" said the Pigeon, in a tone of the deepest contempt. "I've seen a good many little girls in my time, but never one with such a neck as that! No, no! You're a serpent; and there's no use denying it. I suppose you'll be telling me next that you never tasted an egg!"

"I have tasted eggs, certainly," said Alice, who was a very truthful child; "but little girls eat eggs quite as much as serpents do, you know."

"I don't believe it," said the Pigeon; "but if they do, why, then they're a kind of serpent: that's all I can say."

2. 选段一①于 2022 年 8 月 13 日发表于《经济学人》；选

---

① Burning up [N]. The Economist, 2022-08-13 (74) .

段二①是加州大学伯克利大学分校林思·亨青格教授针对该文发表的一篇评论性文章,也发表于《经济学人》。请仔细阅读这两篇文章,并回答下面几个问题:

(1) 选段一的核心观点是什么?作者通过怎样的论证方式得出了这一观点?

(2) 选段二提出了怎样的反对观点?指出了选段一的何种逻辑谬误?

选段一

What is the most famous scene in *Bambi*? Eighty years on from the film's premiere in August 1942, there is only one answer: it is the scene in which Bambi's mother dies. The Walt Disney cartoon—ostensibly about a deer gambolling around an idyllic forest—has traumatized generations of youngsters. What is even more impressive is that the scene doesn't actually exist. Whatever memory viewers might have, the film doesn't explicitly show the death of Bambi's mother.

About 40 minutes in (no, it's not in the first ten minutes, although many share that false memory, too), doe and fawn are

---

① HUNTSINGER L. Fire as a forest management [N]. The Economist, 2022-09-03 (14).

running from unseen hunters through a snowy meadow. A gunshot is heard. Bambi races back to his shelter in "the thicket", only to realise, after a second of elated relief, that he is alone. His majestic father then looms over him in silhouette and murmurs: "Your mother can't be with you any more." And that's that. There are no poignant last words, no mourning period or slow recovery. The film immediately cuts to a tra-la-la-ing song about falling in love in the springtime, and Bambi's mum is never mentioned again. For Bambi, Thumper and their woodland friends, death is just an everyday part of growing up. The film's viewers may be perturbed by this attitude, but the animals aren't.

This brisk lack of sentiment is typical of a film which is far bolder than its fluffy reputation might suggest. Adapted from a novel by Felix Salten, an Austro-Hungarian author, Disney's fifth feature-length cartoon is a gorgeous tapestry of different animation techniques. There is no adventure plot or triumph-over-adversity theme imposed on the art: David Hand, the supervising director, simply made a 70minute chronicle of a wobbly legged deer's learning about life and death.

Watching it now, in the middle of a dangerously hot summer, the most horrifying sequence is the one in which a wildfire consumes the forest. In later Disney cartoons, this sort of eco-catastrophe would be caused by lightning (as in *The Jungle Book*) or by greedy hyenas (*The Lion King*). In *Bambi*, however, humans are squarely to blame. Not that any people are depicted: Bambi is warned of a species called "Man", but, just as Hand omitted the killing of the fawn's mother, he chose not to show any humans on screen.

Instead, the flames from an unattended campfire are blown into a tree, and then an unstoppable blaze turns a green paradise into an inferno. No one in particular is responsible. There is no snarling Captain Hook, Maleficent or Cruella de Vil to reassure viewers that only evildoers destroy the environment. Man in general, it seems, is so careless that he would rather lay waste to nature than go to the effort of putting out a campfire.

Again, the film doesn't have any wailing or gnashing of teeth. No one delivers any speeches about the injustice of it all, and no one expresses the hope that it might not happen again. Wildfires are just one more thing that the animals have got used to. And now humans must get used to them as well: a thought as harrowing as the demise of Bambi's mother.

选段二

I taught a culture and forestry class for many years, and I've seen *Bambi* about 20 times. I appreciated your article on what the Disney classic tells us about eco-disasters ("Burning up", August 13th), but there are some important things to mention about the portrayal of fire. Open woodlands and patchy forests tend to have much higher levels of biodiversity and are more resistant to high severity wildfire, good reasons for making fire and other means of thinning forests part of our management practices. Even in Europe the emphasis on managing dense forests is relatively new. The Black Forest, for example, used to be managed by a form of Swidden, slashing and burning, in the 19th century.

Bambi actually portrays the outcome of a fire very well. After the tragic event, flowers and herbs abound and Bambi's mate has twins. This is not unusual. In the years following a fire there is typically a profusion of forage for deer and elk, and a habitat for an abundance of creatures that simply need more sun. This nutritional burst leads to more young.

Too often we characterize an ecological phenomenon as

bad or good, when in fact it is part of how the ecosystem works. Sometimes a short term "damage" is a long-term benefit, especially if it leads to greater ecosystem resilience and fewer over-fuelled fires that burn everything in their path. I hope that people will come to terms with this, so that the active management of our forests can begin.

3. 阅读本专业的一篇期刊论文，思考该论文的主要结论是什么以及这一结论是通过哪种论证方式得出的。分析该论文的论证逻辑。

第三讲　组　织

上一讲，我们讲了学术写作中的论证逻辑。有了清晰的论证逻辑，接下来，我们要想想组织的事。

着手于组织的具体方法，叶圣陶先生说：

> 为要使各部分环拱于中心，就得致力于裁剪。为要使各部分密合妥适，就得致力于排次。把所有的材料逐步审查，而以是否与总旨一致为标准，这时候自然知所去取，于是检定一致的、必要的，去掉不一致的、不适用的，或者还补充上遗漏的、不容少的，这就是裁剪的功夫。经过剪裁的材料方是可以确信的需用的材料。然后把材料排次起来，而以是否合于论理上的顺序为尺度，这时候自然有所觉知。于是让某部居开端、某部居末梢，某部与某部衔接；而某部与某部之间如其有复叠或罅隙，也会发现出来，并且知道应当怎样去修补。[1]

---

[1] 叶圣陶. 怎样写作 [M]. 北京：中华书局，2007: 13–14.

这段话提到的两个关键点，一个是裁剪，一个是排次。

裁剪是为着论证着想，让论证逻辑凸显出来。比方说，一个实验有千百个步骤，裁剪就是选取对实验可重复至关重要的那些步骤；研究的发现林林总总，裁剪就是呈现和研究问题最相关的结果；多个论据都可以支撑一个小论点时，裁剪就是选取最有说服力的那个。

排次，简而言之，就是先说什么、后说什么，就是整体上的组织架构。学术文章不强调制造惊喜和悬念，排次的原则就是在特定的位置呈现特定的信息，带领读者在可预期的框架下思考。

还拿上一讲的例子说。为了让读者信服我们的论证，我们不能一上来就说：我要开始论证"匈牙利选手应被取消名次"这件事了。如果这样开头，读者会一头雾水：哪来的匈牙利选手？即使有读者了解我们说的是 2022 年北京冬奥会上那个在 1000 米决赛中第一个冲过终点的那个匈牙利选手，仍会质疑：比赛中被取消名次的选手多了，为什么非要研究他呢？因此，我们需要首先告诉读者："匈牙利选手是否应被取消名次"是一个很有价值的、值得一探的科学问题。我们可以从下面几个方面思考：

1. 发生犯规的背景是 2022 年北京冬奥会。奥运会是全世界规模最大、参与人数最多、影响力最大的体育赛事。比赛结果对运动员职业生涯影响重大。

2. 国际滑联为减少比赛过程中无谓的运动员受伤，增强比赛的观赏性，于 2020 年颁布了短道速滑的最新规则。这些规则能否在实际比赛中落地，对其他运动员平日的训练和赛场上的技战术安排具有很强的指导意义。

3. 匈牙利选手若被判犯规，第二个冲过终点的中国选手将获得金牌。裁判在比赛中若偏袒了东道主选手，会影响人们对比赛公平性的认识。

此外，当我们经过一番演绎论证，证明了**匈牙利选手应该被取消比赛名次**后，难免还会遭到另外的质疑。比如，新规则下为什么同样的阻挡情况在某某场和某某场的比赛中没有被判犯规呢？为什么任子威临近终点处的拉拽动作没有被判犯规呢？此时，我们或还需要阐释清楚：

1. 匈牙利选手的阻挡和某某年某某比赛某某人的阻挡是不同的。

2. 匈牙利选手和中国选手在临近终点处的手肘动作的发生时间和作用效果是不同的。

以上这些虽不影响文章大的论证逻辑，但如果论证清楚，有助于读者接受我们核心论证中的"结论"。我们在裁剪和排次时需要考虑这些方面。

学术文体包罗万象。不同的学术文体在排次上有不小的差异。常见的学术文体就包括学位论文、实证研究论文、综述类论文、书评、基金申请书、专利申请书等。相比一一介绍各种学术文体裁剪、排次的细节，不如介绍掌握裁剪、排次的方法。

有一个和八仙之一吕洞宾有关的小故事，说的就是方法的意义。据清人方飞鸿在《广谈助》中记载：

> 一人贫苦特甚，生平虔奉吕祖，祖感其诚，忽降其家；见其赤贫，不胜悯之，因伸一指指其庭中磐石，粲然化为黄金，曰："汝欲之乎？"其人再拜曰："不欲也。"吕祖大喜，谓："子诚如此，便可授予大道。"其人曰："不然，我心欲汝此指头耳。"①

对学术文章的裁剪、排次而言，这个点石成金的指头就是逆向工程法。

逆向工程法是工程学上的一个概念，指的是对一项目标产品进行逆向分析及研究，从而演绎并得出该产品的处理流程、组织结构、功能特性及技术规格等设计要素，以期制作出功能相近、但又不完全一样的产品。

如何在学术写作时应用逆向工程法呢？首先，我们要深入观察和分析已发表的文本范例，尽可能还原作者在谋篇布局时的思路，归纳出自己所在学科中，大家普遍遵守的一些写作模型；其次，在大量的阅读中不断检验、印证自己总结出来的写作模型，逐步完善这个模型，并尝试应用到自己的写作实践中。

以期刊论文为例，我们可以通过对一级和二级标题的观察了

---

① 王利器. 历代笑话集 [G]. 北京：中华书局，2020: 437.

解文章组织架构的基本思路：哪部分在先，哪部分在后。了解排次之后，我们还可以粗略统计一下各级标题下的文字占全篇文字的比例。

具体到摘要、引言、方法、结果、讨论等部分，我们可以展开更深入且细致的观察和分析。以引言为例，我们可观察和分析的点包括：

1. 引言包含几个段落？每个段落讲述的内容是什么？
2. 引言从开头至结尾的叙述，是如何铺展开的？
3. 能否从具体的叙述中抽象出一个写作模型，指导未来的引言写作实践？

下面我们以一篇论文为例，更直观地看看这个分析的过程。这篇发表在《应用化学国际版》（化学类顶级期刊）上的论文研究并验证了一种导电纳米材料包裹产电微生物在提高微生物燃料电池性能方面的作用。下文是一位同学对该论文引言部分的分析，涵盖了上述的三个步骤。

学术论文引言分析
——以《应用化学国际版》上的一篇论文①为例

1. 段落分析

The coating of functional materials onto the surfaces of individual living systems not only protects their bioinformation under harsh environments, but also helps increase their stability and performance as well as introduces more functionalities in bio-related devices including sensing, bioreactors, and microfluidic devices.[1] Moreover, such coating would provide scientists more fundamental information during the study of cell biology. Inspired by biological preservation mechanism, several protective coatings including metal-organic frameworks (MOF), iron-tannate coordination complex, silica and silica-titania have been demonstrated to enhance cellular viability under environmental stresses.[2] In addition, recent studies have already shown that the encapsulation of yeast cells with conducting coatings (e.g. graphene and polydopamine) not only prolongs the cell lifetime but also offers good electrical conductivity.[3]	引言包含三个段落。首段介绍大的研究背景及研究意义。 第一段第一句介绍了研究领域——功能性涂层材料（将其置于首句主语），并介绍了研究该领域几方面的意义（not only…，but also…；as well as；Moreover）。 综述功能性涂层材料这一领域现有的研究，突出这种材料已被证实的优点（通过连接词 In addition，将相关文献整合起来）。

---

① SONG R B, WU Y C, LIN Z Q, et al. Living and conducting: Coating individual bacterial cells with in situ formed polypyrrole [J]. Angewandte Chemie International Edition, 2017, 56: 10516-10520.

（续表）

Although such coatings possess many advantages and can introduce additional functionalities to cells, the potential applications of these surface-modified cells have not been fully exploited. Thus, advancing the development of some important research fields like microbial fuel cells (MFCs) by slickly integrating basic functions of biological units with intrinsic properties of surface coatings is highly desirable.	Although 引导的一句，承上启下，重在揭示这类材料的应用价值尚未充分开发（not been fully exploited）。紧承研究空白，提出本文研究大目标（Thus, … is highly desirable）。
MFCs are typical bioelectrochemical systems (BESs) that harness the metabolism of exoelectrogenic bacteria to harvest electricity from organic substrates, and have attracted continuous attention due to their great potential for simultaneously satisfying the need of sustainable energy production and wastewater treatment.[4] Although huge improvements have been achieved in recent years, MFCs are still far from reaching the level of practical applications due to their relatively low power density.[5] Generally, the extracellular electron transfer (EET) between exoelectrogens and anodes is keenly considered as a key step to determine the power output of MFCs.[6] In the past, extensive studies have been devoted to tailor the anode for improving the exoelectrogen-anode interactions and thus the EET efficiency.[7] One strategy is to enhance the surface properties of anodes[4,8] and	引言第二段聚焦微生物燃料电池（MFCs）这一具体的研究领域，并指出具体的研究空白。首句介绍 MFCs 的相关背景知识，以及该应用领域为何得到持续的研究关注。Although 引导的一句，揭示了目前 MFCs 实际应用存在的问题（far from …）及原因（due to …）。 介绍为了解决 MFC 实际应用存在的问题，前人（In the past）做了哪些努力（One strategy is …, and the other way is …）

	(续表)
the other way is to fabricate nanomaterials with sophisticated structures as anodes.[9] However, in both research directions, bacteria attach onto the anode in a naturally growth manner, which limits bacteria loading to some extent.[10] In view of this disadvantage, researches on the anodes of MFC have begun to flourish in fabricating electroactive hybrid biofilms, as they possess high bacterial cell density and enhanced EET efficiencies.[11] However, it is inevitable that some of the bacterial cells in electroactive hybrid biofilms cannot be directly associated with conductive materials. In this case, the electron propagation between these bacterial cells and anodes is only through adjacent nonconductive bacteria,[12] resulting in a reduction in EET efficiency. To address this issue, employing conducting-nanomaterial-coated bacteria should be a promising strategy in such engineering MFCs because this arrangement would allow the electron transport more efficiently from inner cells to the electrode.	介绍以往方法/策略的不足之处。 鉴于不足，相关研究是如何突破的。 However 引导的一句，凸显仍有需要突破的不足之处（研究空白）。 指出本文为取得突破，拟提出一种解决思路。
Since polypyrrole (PPy) has been widely demonstrated as a biocompatible and excellent electrical conducting medium,[13] the modification of bacterial cells with PPy is anticipated to improve the electrical conductivity of bacterial cells without reducing their viability. Therefore, in this research, we employ this system to prove the possibility of coating in situ formed PPy onto the surfaceof individual bacterial cells.	引言第三段介绍本文的工作。 首句交代本文为什么选用 polypyrrole (PPy) 这一功能性涂层材料。 大致介绍本文做的工作。

(续表)

Specifically, *Shewanella oneidensis* MR-1 was chosen as a model exoelectrogen because the formation of PPy on the surface of bacterial cells can enhance the affinitive mechanical contact with c-type cytochromes, which locate on the outer membrane of bacterial cells and play an important function to transfer electrons from *S. oneidensis* MR-1 to anodes.[14] Our results clearly indicated that the direct contact-based EET process and bioelectricity generation are superior to that of the unmodified exoelectrogen. Furthermore, with the same procedure, PPy can also be coated on the surface of three other individual bacterial cells, including *Escherichia coli*, *Ochrobacterium anthropic* and *Streptococcus thermophilus*. In all cases, PPy can improve the conductivity of bacterial cells while maintaining cell viability.	介绍取得的主要结果，凸显研究价值。

2. 写作思路

　　这篇论文的引言部分首先定位了一个大的研究领域——功能性涂层材料，列举了这种材料的优点和在许多领域的应用价值，说明了这类研究的重要性。接着，作者综述了以往的一些相关研究，指出这种材料的应用价值未得到充分开发，由此提出本研究大的研究目标。

　　引言第二段首先聚焦到一个具体的应用领域——微生物燃料电池，并说明了其重要的应用价值以及在实际应用中存在的瓶颈。

接下来，作者介绍了突破此瓶颈的关键限制性因素，并由此综述了以往研究发展出来的两种策略。接着，作者指出了这两种策略的局限性，介绍了以往研究是如何突破局限的，以及仍然存在的不足。通过层层递进，提出本文的研究目标。相较第一段提出的研究目标，此时的研究目标更加具体和有针对性。

第三段聚焦本项研究，说明本项研究如何弥补了现有的空白。开头首先交代了选择 polypyrrole (PPy) 作为涂层材料的原因，然后大致介绍了本文的工作以及取得的重要结果，突出了研究取得的突破。

引言部分呈现了漏斗形结构：从大的研究领域到小的研究方向，从已有的发现到尚未解决的问题。通过逻辑上的层层递进，既说明了本研究的研究理据，也为下文的展开做好了铺垫。

3. 写作模型

结构要素	说　明
研究领域及研究意义	本期刊是世界领先的化学类顶级期刊之一，对创新性要求高，且需具有一定的理论深度，因此首段从 coating of functional materials 介绍起，符合期刊定位。如果目标期刊偏向于应用，则可直接从应用研究 microbial fuel cells (MFCs)（本文第二段）介绍起。
综述已有文献，指出研究空白，确立研究目标	引言部分的重点。文献综述由远及近，研究空白由大到小，体现科学知识积累呈螺旋式上升的特点。研究目标随研究空白逐步呈现，从大方向到小问题。
介绍本研究	指出研究的创新点（交代在众多涂层材料中选择了 PPy 的依据）；呈现主要研究结果，使读者较早得知研究全貌，提高阅读效率。

按此思路分析文章的剩余部分，我们就得到了论文整体的写作模型。这个模型很抽象，和内容无关，是论文的骨架。但有了这样的骨架，论文就能"立"得起来。迄今，学者们基于众多语料，提供了一些论文写作模型，可为学术论文提供普遍意义上的参考，但自己走一遍这个过程，能在不知不觉中领会排次的一些精微之处，也能体会所在学科的独特性。

我在本讲文末附了几位同学对论文引言部分的思考，从中可见他们从"逆向工程法"中获得的对论文引言一些精微的认识。

为了排次的意识建立、能力养成，自己动笔时也不妨在纸面上写个提纲或者心中打个腹稿。席尔瓦教授在《如何文思泉涌》①中说，列提纲不是写作的序曲，列提纲就是写作本身。

有同学恐怕要问：严格地遵循排次，这样写出的学术文章不是八股文吗？我们能不能有创新呢？的确，有人称学术文章为"洋八股"，说的就是学术写作高度结构化的特征。但这样的特征，是不是如同希腊神话中"普洛克路斯忒斯之床"（Procrustean Bed），极大地束缚了我们的手脚呢？

我想，学术写作的高度结构化，是一种法度。熟练掌握了篇章的组织方式，亦有探索自在的可能。正如唐楷，"楷"字是模范、法式的意思，我们从小学习楷书，学的大概也是法则、规矩。法度之下，是书家各自的性情。颜真卿的天真雄浑、欧阳询的平正险劲、褚遂良的空灵飞动、虞世南的虚静谦和。他们没有被法

---

① SILVA P J. How to write a lot: A practical guide to productive academic writing [M]. Second Edition. New York: American Psychological Association, 2018: 78.

度所束缚,而是以法度得到了自由。

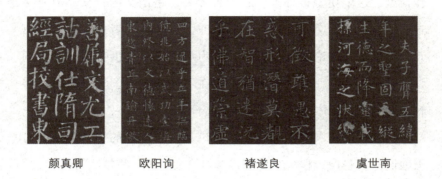

颜真卿　　　　欧阳询　　　　褚遂良　　　　虞世南

更进一步说,法度就是自由。篇章之内有了谨严的法度,我们在阅读中,就不必线性地从头读到尾,而可以根据清晰的结构所提供的"路标",有目的性地获取信息;写作时,也不必从前至后徐徐展开,而可以根据结构中每一部分特有的功能,灵活地安排写作顺序。

附：

　　我的专业是网络空间安全，我的研究方向是人工智能安全。

　　我觉得学术论文的引言是一个纺锤体。因为在引言部分，作者会首先介绍该问题目前的研究进展与背景，紧接着介绍文章的章节安排、相关工作、实验之类的内容——这一部分内容较为丰富，类似纺锤体的中间部分。最后则是一些展望或是补充性的说明。整个引言部分的开头和结尾都较为精简，中间部分最为丰富，因此我认为引言部分就像是一个纺锤体。

高培杰（2021级硕士研究生）

　　我的专业是网络空间安全，我的研究方向是物联网安全。

　　我觉得学术论文的引言是一个椭圆，原因如下：一篇完整、优秀的论文引言应以核心论点为中心，进而向各个方向延伸，娓娓道来。据此，作者可以表达自己的观点和贡献，读者可以理解整篇文章的背景和旨归。在这种理想状态下，引言部分可以形象比喻为"圆"。然而，由于作者受限于认知水平、文章篇幅或其他因素，在撰写过程中，总有意无意地进行详略安排，凸显文章的主要贡献和重要意义，在一定程度上简略文章的次要发现或不足之处，因此实际中，引言部分更像"椭圆"。

郗来乐（2021级硕士研究生）

　　我的专业是材料物理与化学，我的研究方向是宽禁带半导体材料与器件。

　　我觉得学术论文的引言是一串冰糖葫芦，写引言就像是一个为竹签穿上一颗又一颗山楂。在材料科学领域，材料的基本性质是基础，它决定着材料的应用潜能，就像是冰糖葫芦上的第一颗山楂；材料在应用的过程中遇到的技术难点是第二颗山楂，它不仅向我们展现出过往研究中的不足，还指出了对这种材料进一步研究的方向；目前国内外的研究现状是第三颗山楂，它展示出了攻克上述技术难点的办法，以及有待进步的地方；材料的生长技术是第四颗山楂，它阐述了材料在生长的过程中需要用到的方法和仪器；对我们取得的研究成果的描述是最后一颗山楂。

　　对引言进行的修改就像是一个熬糖浆的过程，只有经过字斟句酌的修改，才能给冰糖葫芦裹上晶莹剔透、香甜可口的糖浆，让读者享受到我们的科研成果。

多亦威（2021级硕士研究生）

本讲练习

1. 请用"逆向工程法"分析一篇本领域论文的讨论部分（Discussion Section），提炼写作思路，并尝试给出这一部分的写作模型。

2. 请用"逆向工程法"分析五篇本领域论文的摘要部分（Abstract Section），提炼写作思路，并尝试给出这一部分的写作模型。

3. 请用"逆向工程法"分析论文之外的一种学术文体（如书评、项目申请书、实验报告、论文评审意见等），提炼写作思路，并尝试给出这种文体的写作模型。

第四讲　流　动

提到流动（flow）这个词，大家想到了什么？立即映现在你头脑中的画面是什么？

有同学想到了河流、身体中的血液、看不见的波，有同学想到了舞蹈、书法，还有同学想到了交通堵塞。对的，交通堵塞就是车辆正常的流动受到了阻滞。

学术写作中的流动指的是语义在句子和句子、段落和段落之间的通达。叶圣陶和夏丏尊先生在《文心》① 中说："作文和说话是一样的，在承接和转折的地方最要留心。一句里边有几个词儿不得当，还不过是一句的毛病；承接和转折的地方弄错了，那就把一段的意思搅糊涂了。"

认知写作学的创始者阳志平说："文章之于大脑，如同布料之于熨斗。当你的写作如丝绸般平滑，读者只需将熨斗温度调到最低，投入一点点大脑能量，就能轻松愉快地开始一场冒险。如果我们的文章是粗糙的干棉布，读者就需要将熨斗温度调到最高，投入大量的大脑能量，还经常得忍受难看的褶皱与乱窜的水

---

① 夏丏尊，叶圣陶. 文心 [M]. 北京：开明出版社，2017: 26.

蒸气。"①

下面我们从真实的文章入手,通过具体的语言事实看看如丝绸般平滑的文章是如何写成的。这次给同学们选的文章来自一个很有名的杂志《英国医学期刊》,是医学领域很知名的期刊。这个期刊每年在圣诞节前后会出一期特刊,刊发一些话题有趣,短小精练,但也不失学术严谨的文章。

2014年的圣诞特刊里有这么一篇文章,题目是《达尔文奖:愚蠢行为的性别差异》②。达尔文奖每年会颁发给那些"通过愚蠢的方式自我毁灭,为人类的进化做出深远贡献"的人。这篇文章统计了1995至2014年间所有获奖者的性别。卡方检验显示,男性的获奖比例远远大于女性。作者给出了对这个结果的解释。

接下来,我们从写作的角度,仔细地看看这篇文章中语义的流动是如何实现的。

首先,是逻辑连接词(logical connectives)的使用。这是直观上最容易发现的。合理使用逻辑连接词,上下两句话的关系就明晰了。比如,作者举了一些例子来界定"愚蠢行为"。这些例子中不乏生词,但示例连接词(如 for example, for instance, examples include)清晰地表明了上下句的逻辑关系。除了示例,作者还用到了对比、增补、转折等逻辑连接词,我们一一举例。

---

① 阳志平. 读了这四本书, 你会更懂写作. [EB/OL]. (2022-03-26) [2022-11-01]. https://blog.openmindclub.com/2022/03/26/YangZhiPing-WriteBookList/

② LENDREM B A D, LENDREM D W, GRAY A, et al. The Darwin awards: Sex differences in idiotic behavior [J]. British Medical Journal, 2014, 349: g7094.

（1）对比

Darwin Awards are unlikely to be awarded to individuals who shoot themselves in the head while demonstrating that a gun is unloaded. This occurs too often and is classed as an accident. In contrast, candidates shooting themselves in the head to demonstrate that a gun is loaded may be eligible for a Darwin Award.（用 In contrast 对比会被授予达尔文奖和不会被授予达尔文奖的候选者）

（2）增补

One of the weaknesses is the retrospective nature of the data collection. ... In addition, there may be some selection bias within the Darwin Awards Committee.（在指出本文第一个弱点的基础上，用 In addition 引出第二个弱点）

（3）转折

Sex differences in risk seeking behavior, emergency hospital admissions, and mortality are well documented. However, little is known about sex differences in idiotic risk-taking behavior.（用 However 引出前人研究的空白）

有同学或许会有疑问：还有一类表因果的连接词，比如"因为"（because, since, as, for），"所以"（therefore, so, as a result），怎么在文章中一次都没有出现呢？仔细重读文章会发现，在引言和讨论部分，实际上都有表达因果逻辑的句子，只是作者没有选取逻辑连接词，而是选用了下面的方式：

（1）Some of these differences may be <u>attributable to</u> cultural and socioeconomic factors.（引言部分）

（2）However, sex differences in risk seeking behavior have been reported from an early age, raising questions about the extent to which these behaviors can be <u>attributed</u> purely to social and cultural differences.（引言部分）

（3）In addition, alcohol may play an important part in many of the events <u>leading to</u> a Darwin Award.（讨论部分）

作者如此选择，是否仅是个人用词的偏好呢？还是反映了某种学科特点？我把这个问题留给大家。不妨把上述三句中的 may/may be, can be, the extent to which 也划出来，想想这些词起到了什么样的作用。

实现语义的流通，除了逻辑连接词，还可以借助这/这些（this/these）。我们先来看例子：

(1) Northcutt cites a number of worthy candidates[17-21]. These include the thief…; the man…; and the terrorist… (指代 candidates)

(2) For the statistical analysis, we excluded those awards shared by both sexes—usually couples. This meant that under the null hypothesis we assumed Darwin Awards were equally likely to be awarded to males and females according to their approximate distribution in the overall population (50:50). (指代前面一整句)

(3) This paper reports a marked sex difference in Darwin Award winners: males are significantly more likely to receive the award than females ($P<0.0001$). We discuss some of the reasons for this difference. (指代 sex difference)

(4) Sex differences in mortality and admissions to hospital emergency departments have been well documented[1-7], and hypotheses put forward to account for these differences. These studies confirm that males are more at risk than females. (指代上文提及的 1—7 文献中的研究)

(5) There are anecdotal data supporting MIT, but to date there has been no systematic analysis of sex differences in idiotic risk-taking behavior. In this paper we present evidence in support of this hy-

pothesis using data on idiotic behaviors demonstrated by winners of the Darwin Award[17-21]. (指代上文提及的 MIT 假说)

(6) This paper reports marked sex differences in the distribution of Darwin Award winners, with males much more likely to receive an award. This finding is entirely consistent with male idiot theory (MIT)[16-20] and supports the hypothesis that men are idiots and idiots do stupid things. (指代上文提及的结果)

(7) Northcutt invokes a group selectionist, "survival of the species" argument, with individuals selflessly removing themselves from the gene pool. We believe this view to be flawed, but we do think this phenomenon probably deserves an evolutionary explanation. (分别指代 Northcutt "自然选择论" 的观点和个体以愚蠢的方式自我毁灭的现象)

This/these 的使用可以分为两类情况。一类是作为代词使用（例1、例2），一类是后面加一个名词（例3至例8）。通常，this/these 指代的对象非常明确，不会引起歧义的时候，可用作代词单独使用。而 this/these 加名词，可以明确地告诉读者 this/these 指代的是什么，如例3中的 this difference 指代上文提及的 sex difference，例4中的 these studies 指代上文提及的7篇文献。此外，this/these 之后的名词可具有一定的抽象度，用以概括前句所述，如例5

中的 hypothesis，例 6 中的 finding 和例 7 中的 view 及 phenomenon。

实现语义流通的第三种方式，是更普遍的，但往往容易被我们忽略的方式。这种方式我叫它交叠（overlapping），指的是后一句使用了和前句一致、相近或高度相关的词语。这样的例子在文中比比皆是：

（1）This paper reviews the data on winners of the Darwin Award over a 20-year period (1995—2014). Winners of the Darwin Award must eliminate themselves from the gene pool in such an idiotic manner that their action ensures one less idiot will survive.

（2）To qualify, nominees must improve the gene pool by eliminating themselves from the human race using astonishingly stupid methods. Northcutt cites a number of worthy candidates [17-21].

（3）However, this study has limitations. One of the weaknesses is the retrospective nature of the data collection.

（4）Our analysis included only confirmed accounts verified by the Darwin Awards Committee. Urban legends and unverified accounts were excluded.

（5）In addition, there may be some kind of reporting bias. Idiotic male candidates may be more newsworthy than idiotic female Darwin Award candidates.

例 1 中，第一句 winners of the Darwin Award 是在宾语补足语的位置上，说明本项研究数据的来源。下一句将 winners of Darwin Award 用作主语，进一步介绍 winners of Darwin Award 的评选条件。重复，仅仅是简单的重复，我们就能感到语义的贯通。例 2 至例 4 中，作者没有一字不差地重复，而在上下句选用了同义词（如例 2 中的 nominees 和 candidates, 例 3 中的 limitations 和 weaknesses），或者反义词（如例 4 中的 included 和 excluded, confirmed 和 unverified）。例 5 的例子稍微特殊一点，这里的交叠既不是通过一字不差的重复，也不是通过同、反义词，但我们读到前句的 reporting 和后句的 newsworthy 时，能感到这两个词的高度关联，这里的连贯感是通过选用"同一语义场"的词来实现的。

以上我们给出的例子，基本只涉及两句话。下面我们通过一个较长的段落，来看看实现语义流通的三种方式（逻辑连接词，这/这些，交叠）的综合运用。

An area where positive psychology is making inroads is in the health industry, particularly in the area of dealing with serious illness. One such illness is cancer, a life-threatening disease that directly or indirectly affects a large portion of the Australian population. The seriousness of this issue is highlighted by the fact that one in two Australian men and one in three Australian women will be diagnosed with cancer by the age of eighty-five (Cancer Council Australia, 2016). Importantly, a cancer diagnosis, along with treatments and side effects, has the potential to significantly reduce an individual's quality of life with substantial impact not only physically, but also on social and emotional health. These psychological impacts of cancer have traditionally been treated through problem-fixing initiatives (Grau & Vives, 2014); however, evidence is increasingly pointing towards the efficacy of positive psychology interventions. This paper examines ways in which such interventions are used and processes that they may positively influence the psychosocial health and well-being of those living with a cancer diagnosis.

这段话讲的是积极心理学在疾病领域的应用价值。作者开篇直奔主题：积极心理学正进军到人类健康领域，尤其是对抗重病方面。首句以 illness 结尾，第二句以 one such illness 开头，通过重复，实现语义贯通。第二句，作者把目光聚焦到一类重症，即癌症上，并描述了癌症的巨大危害。第三句开头的 this issue 所指代的，恰恰就是第二句提到的癌症。第三句征引 Cancer Council Australia 发布的数据（到 85 岁，澳大利亚一半的男性和三分之一的女性都会被确诊癌症），揭示了癌症的严重危害。第四句主语中的 diagnosis 和第三句的 diagnosed，第五句主语中的 impacts 和第四句中的 impact 形成完美的照应，词性的变化似乎让语言的流动性更佳。

四、五两句，段落所述话题的重心由癌症的诊断转向癌症对人的心理影响。第五句的中间，作者用 however 对比了在癌症病人的心理干预方面较为传统的方式和最新的方式（通过积极心理学来实施干预）。本段末句的 such interventions 照应了第五句中的 interventions，将行文方向引向积极心理学的临床干预。

这个选段只用了一处逻辑连接词（however），但我们读下来，能感到作者的行文逻辑是非常清晰的。我们平日的写作容易强加逻辑连接词（没有明显逻辑关系的前后两句硬加了逻辑连接词）、缺失逻辑连接词（有明显逻辑关系的前后两句没有用逻辑连接词）和误用逻辑连接词（如有因果关系的前后两句间用了表增补的连接词）。请大家仔细研读上面这个选段，好好体会作者如何通过代词、词汇的重复以及连接词的适当使用来实现段落之内语义的自然流动。

以上我们对语义流通的讨论，集中在句子和段落内部。下面我们略作扩展，看看段落和段落之间的语义流通是如何实现的。

玛丽-凯特·麦基在《写作提高一点点》一书[①]中提出"指针句"（pointer sentence）这个概念。她说，从上一段到下一段，要为读者搭建起一个桥梁，使他们明晰前后两段的逻辑承接关系。

指针句可以在上一段的句末，给读者一个信号，让他们对接下来的内容有所预期；也可以在下一段之首，概括上文、引出下文。下面举两个例子。

---

① MACKEY M-K. Write better right now: The reluctant writer's guide to confident communication and self-assured style [M]. New Jersey: Career Press, 2017: 204.

As classroom-based action research usually takes off from a specific teaching context and involves systematic collection and analysis of real-life data over time to see whether changes take place, the following subsections introduce the study's instructional context as well as ways to evaluate teaching/learning outcomes.

这是我自己论文①中的一个例子。在写作这一部分的初稿时，我列的写作框架是：

2. 方法
行动研究的定义和特点
2.1 教学情境
2.2 参与者
2.3 评估方案

初稿中 2.1 小节之前，介绍"行动研究的定义和特点"一段的末句是"Classroom-based action research usually takes off from a specific teaching context and involves systematic collection and analysis of real-life data over time to see whether changes take place"。2.1 小节的开头一句是"The students in the study were enrolled in a credit-bearing EAP reading and writing course for non-English majors"。

---

① DU Y. Adopting critical-pragmatic pedagogy to address plagiarism in a Chinese context: An action research [J]. Journal of English for Academic Purposes, 2022, 57, 101112.

审校时，我发现这两段的过渡很生硬。于是，我重新阅读了前一段的末句，发现这句话提及的内容和后面三个小节存在关联，某种意义上就是要写后面三个小节的理据。于是，我在这句话前面加上了 As 这一逻辑连接词，后面加上了"the following subsections introduce the study's instructional context as well as ways to evaluate teaching/learning outcomes"，这样一来，前后两段的过渡就流畅、自然了。

第二个例子来自同一篇论文的讨论部分。当初在构思这部分时，我的思路如下：

4. 讨论
本文的价值和贡献
本文不足之处 1（Firstly）
本文不足之处 2（Secondly）
本文不足之处 3（Finally）
重述本文的价值和贡献

下面是两段初稿和终稿的比较。

初稿：Firstly, I recognized in retrospect a few missed opportunities to move the discussion deeper.

终稿：Although various in-class activities prompting students' active engagement with academic source-attribution conventions were tried, I recognized in retrospect a few missed opportunities to move discussions deeper.

初稿：Secondly, it is very important to trace students' development of critical awareness as the action research progresses.

终稿：In addition to studying students' evaluation for the teaching unit and their actual attribution performance, it is very important to trace students' development of critical awareness as the action research progresses.

初稿中，三点不足各自成段，并使用了 Firstly，Secondly 和 Finally 三个引导词。这样的列举方式虽然清晰，但显得有些生硬，而且似乎让不足之处突显了。终稿中，我将不足之处 1 之前的 Firstly 和不足之处 2 之前的 Secondly 去掉，使用指针句让对本文贡献的描述自然、流畅地转向对本文局限的描述。下面再举一例：

初稿：To sum up, this three-year action research responds to an urgent need for critical-pragmatic EAP to focus on implementation, demonstrating how a critical-pragmatic approach can be employed in specific institutional settings through well-designed classroom activities.

终稿：Despite the limitations outlined above, this three-year action research responds to an urgent need for critical-pragmatic EAP to focus on implementation, demonstrating how a critical-pragmatic approach can be employed in specific institutional settings through well-designed classroom activities.

初稿中，讨论部分的末段以"To sum up"作结，而在终稿中，我改成了"Despite the limitations outlined above"。修改之后，不仅较好地承接了上文列出的三点不足，也通过让步状语的使用，让读者把关注点放在这一复合句的主句，也就是本文的贡献和价值上。

在这一讲中，我们了解了如何让语义在句子和句子之间，段落和段落之间自然地流动。思维跳跃是人类大脑比较舒适的状态，我们应该都有和另一个人谈事情，谈着谈着就跑题了的经验；思维跳跃也是大脑高度兴奋时很容易出现的状态，比如得到一个大大的喜讯时，我们走路都不能平稳，容易像小孩子一样连蹦带跳起来。

而学术写作强调的是思维的线性推进。读到一篇句与句、段与段过渡平稳的文章，大概如同坐上了一辆平稳驾驶的车。在远处看到红灯时，司机缓缓地踩下刹车；前方需要转弯时，司机提前降速；遇到大雾、沙尘、暴雨等极端天气，司机也会开启相应的信号灯，示意往来车辆。

当我们写作时，不要吝于给读者一些明显的指引吧。否则，他们也许真的会"晕车"呐。

本讲练习

1. 下面一个选段来自一篇关于新型冠状病毒抗体疫苗开发的研究论文[①]的引言部分。请分析本段落句与句的承接关系和实现语义流动的方式。

①Pandemics represent a major threat to global health. ②The coronavirus SARS-CoV-2 has given rise to one of the worst still ongoing pandemics in recent history, COVID-19. ③As of June 2021, the virus had infected more than 181 million individuals and caused almost four million deaths globally. ④The regulatory agencies approved vaccines with unprecedented speed, but their availability remains limited, particularly in low-income countries. ⑤Moreover, the observation of repeated infections within one year (Dao et al., 2020; Huang et al., 2020) suggests that not all individuals develop a protective immune response and that not everyone will respond sufficiently and sustainably to the vaccinations either. ⑥The situation worsened with the occurrence of even more virulent and transmissible

---

① GÜTTLER T, AKSU M, DICKMANNS A, et al. Neutralization of SARS-CoV-2 by highly potent, hyperthermostable, and mutation-tolerant nanobodies [J]. The EMBO Journal, 2021, 40(19), e107985. https://doi.org/10.15252/embj.2021107985

strains, such as Alpha/UK/B.1.1.7 carrying the strain-characte-ring N501Y Spike mutation or the Beta/South African strain B. 1.351. ⑦This raises the need for the continued development of efficient therapies and vaccines with long-lasting efficacy to combat COVID-19. ⑧Therapeutic approaches that interfere with SARS-CoV-2 genome replication, e.g., using the nucleoside analog Remdesivir, showed only moderate if any efficacy in clinical trials so far (Beigel et al., 2020; Spinner et al., 2020). ⑨One reason is the inefficient inhibition of the viral RNA polymerase (Kokic et al., 2021) but perhaps also that the compound cannot prevent the initial infection of cells. ⑩Therefore, it would be desirable to neutralize SARS-CoV-2 before it can enter and infect cells.

2. 请举出本专业的一篇期刊论文中三处使用指针句的实例，并分析"指针句"如何帮助一个段落更好地过渡到了下一个段落。

3. 下面一个段落来自学生课程论文的引言部分。请修改画线句，使之与前后句（段）的衔接更加紧密，流畅性更好。

In college canteen, rarely do we manage to prevent spilling. After crying out "Oh! Too much soup I carried", we may promise ourselves to hold less soup and to walk more carefully next time. However, the consideration and exploration of the soup-spilling phenomenon can go further — "In what postures does it spill out most?", "Why does it spill out?", "What measures should we take to avoid spillage?" This paper will explore the underlying physical mechanism of spillage and propose a practical method to reduce it.

The question "why does coffee spill" has been answered in previous studies. Liquid resonance and hand postures are recognized as critical factors. According to Peter et al. (2019), people can perceive and predict liquid dynamics like liquids-splashing, squirting, gushing, sloshing, soaking, dripping, draining, trickling, pooling, and pouring. This indicates that if one intentionally changes the way holding something, the possibility of spillage may be reduced; Han (2016) found that holding a cup with the "claw hand" posture leads to significant alternatives in the driving force frequency spectrum, suggesting a method to suppress resonance. Apart from that, he also observed when the time span is greatly extended, there will be a conspicuous shift in the frequency spectrum. To explain spillage in a physical way, Mayer and Krechetnikov (2012) chose speeds, accelerations and regimes of walking as variables of their experiments. They adopted an image analysis program written in MATLAB, and set up a physical and mathematical model. The results show that the two main reasons why we spill coffee are large acceleration and resonance with the cup's natural frequency or mid of natural frequency due to the chirped frequency phenomenon.

第五讲　炼　句

句子是写作的基本单位。落笔书写时，盘旋在我们脑海里、紧要解决的问题一定是：下一个句子怎么写？

同样的信息，有太多种表达的可能性。我在写上一讲的一个句子时，心里浮现出好几个版本。

"逻辑连接词的合理使用会让上下两句话的关系变得明晰。"

"逻辑连接词的合理使用使上下两句话的关系变得明晰了。"

"合理使用逻辑连接词会让上下两句话的关系变得明晰。"

"合理使用逻辑连接词就明晰了上下两句话的关系。"

"合理使用逻辑连接词，上下两句话的关系就明晰了。"

福楼拜曾对莫泊桑说："无论你所要的是什么，真正能够表现它的句子只有一个，真正适用的动词和形容词也只有一个，就是那最准确的一句，最准确的一个动词和形容词。其他类似的都很多。而你必须把这唯一的句子、唯一的动词、唯一的形容词找出来。"[1]

我们如何把这"唯一的句子"找出来呢？这一讲，我们就从

---

[1] 莫泊桑. 两兄弟 [M]. 王振孙, 译. 上海：上海译文出版社，2002: 281-282.

句子类型和句中信息位置的选择这两个方面谈谈句子的写作和锤炼。

（一）句子类型的选择

英文句子按照句法结构大体可以分为三类：简单句、并列句、复合句。我们稍作回顾。

简单句是只包含一个主谓结构的句子，如：

Simple sentences are not necessarily short.

并列句包含两个或两个以上主谓结构小句，且各小句连接较为紧密、重要性相当。并列句小句之间通常用并列连词①或分号来连接，如：

I bought a book on academic writing, for it would be useful for my paper publication.

复合句包含两个或两个以上主谓结构的小句，其中有一个或多个主谓结构充当整个句子的某一个（些）成分②。和并列句不

---

① 通常把最常用的并列连词合成为 FANBOYS (for, and, nor, but, or, yet, so)，方便记忆。

② 充当定语的句子叫定语从句（attributive clause），充当状语的句子叫状语从句 (adverbial clause)，充当主语、宾语、表语或同位语的句子叫名词性从句 (nominal clause)。

同，复合句中的各小句重要性并不相当，而是有明显的主从之分，如：

> After writing a complex sentence, you need to check whether the sentence highlights the information you intend to highlight.

那么，学术写作中哪类句子是主流呢？简单句、并列句还是复合句？可能你心中已经浮现出了一个答案。同学们不必急于回答，不妨拿出一小段学术文章仔细观察、做个统计，把答案填到下面这张表里。

句子类型	简单句	并列句	复合句	总计
数量				

通过观察、统计得出一个总体的印象后，我们再通过一些例子，说说句子类型的选择。先来比较一下下面两句话。

例1：The camera takes good pictures.

例2：The camera takes good pictures, and its price is reasonable.

"这个相机照相效果不错"在例1、例2都提到了。例1是简单句，只承载了这一个信息；例2是并列句，前后两个小句地位相当，共同支撑起了整个句子的分量，不过这也意味着，和例1相同信息的分量被句子的另一半分散了。因此我们在写文章时，不必盲目追求复杂的句子。从信息接收的角度来看，该用简单句而使用了并列句，简单句中的信息分量就被大大地削弱了。

再来比较一下下面两句话。

例1：The course textbook was compiled by a team of teaching faculties, and the target users are students of low-to-intermediate level English proficiency.

例2：The course textbook, compiled by a team of teaching faculties, was designed and targeted at students of low-to-intermediate level English proficiency.

例1和例2两句所包含的信息是一样的。例1使用的是并列句，旨在强调前后两句话的信息同等重要；而例2用过去分词做定语，真正的信息重点在后半句。换言之，如果我们想强调的信息是后半句，而选择了例1中的并列句这一句型，一定程度上会降低信息传递的效率。

在同学们平时的作业、课程和毕业论文中，我还发现了过度使用复合句，尤其是定语从句的现象。有一年毕业季评审硕士论文时，我发现一篇一万多字的论文中出现了80次which，也就是大概200个单词里就出现一次which。这是一个什么概念呢？一般英文论文的一个段落的长度是260个单词左右，这样看来，平均每一段都会出现一次 which。我把这种现象称之为"习惯性使用 which",就是不知道句子怎么写下去的时候,就会使用 which。

这里我们需要想一想,定语从句的本质是什么?它是在句中做定语,修饰一个名词或代词。我们看看《哈利·波特》第一部中描写邓布利多的这段话:

> He was tall, thin, and very old, judging by the silver of his hair and beard, which were both long enough to tuck into his belt. He was wearing long robes, a purple cloak that swept the ground, and high-heeled, buckled boots. His blue eyes were light, bright, and sparkling behind half-moon spectacles and his nose was very long and crooked, as though it had been broken at least twice. ①

这段话共有三句。前两句如果不看 which 和 that 后面的部分,都是简单句,而有了 which 和 that,这两句成为了复合句中的定语

---

① ROWLING J K. Harry Potter and the Sorcerer's Stone [M]. New York: Scholastic, 1999: 6.

从句。第一句中的 which 修饰头发和胡子，第二句中的 that 修饰披风。有了这样的修饰，邓布利多的形象亲切可感，which 和 that 实际上起到的都是形容词的作用。

既然是修饰，为什么不能直接用一个形容词而需长长的从句呢？是因为作者没有找到单个的形容词可以表达同样的意思，所以需要一个句子。这是定语从句比较本质的东西。学术论文中，我们不需要那么多的修饰。比如，实验中用到了试管，我们恐怕不需要告诉读者这个试管是很轻的、透明的、拿在手里可能会有点凉的。所以，句子的类型并不是越复杂越好，较为复杂的句子类型（并列句、复合句），一定是有其相应的较为复杂的表意需要。

句子的类型也关乎文章的节奏。一篇节奏感好的文章，就像把各种音符放进一首曲子，展示出急缓、张弛的变化之美。不过这是较高的要求了。刚开始学术写作，句型的选择主要考虑的还是表意的需要。日后可以从变化和节奏的角度稍加考虑。

（二）句中信息的位置

我们通常会在有明显空间概念的场景中考虑位置这件事。比如拍一幅照片，我们会考虑哪里是画面的视觉中心；装饰新家，我们会考虑如何布局家具最为妥当；摆一桌菜，我们会考虑把不同菜品放在合适的位置。

我们写的文章也是占据了空间的。这一点显而易见，因而也常常被我们忽视。紧接着的一个问题是：我们在学术写作中需不需要考虑信息的位置呢？

　　学术文章承载的科学发现与论证过程通常十分复杂，读者面对一个复杂的科学研究，往往需要消耗巨大的认知能量。这就要求作者能有效地传递信息：一句话中强调的信息和读者感受到的信息重点是一致的。口头表达中，我们可以通过多种多样的方式去表达重点信息：视觉上，可通过眼神和手势；听觉上，可以通过声音的大小和节奏。还有这几年很流行的：重要的事情说三遍。笔头表达中，我们偶尔可以通过加黑、加粗、加着重号等方式强调重点信息，但对于绝大部分重点信息的强调，需要借助信息位置的合理安排。

　　首先请同学们想想，一段文字的什么地方最容易引起人们的视觉注意，在某种程度上和加黑、加粗、加着重号的效果相似？没错，是句与句的连接处。由于有了标点符号的区隔，一句话的开头和结尾，让人印象更为深刻。

　　因此，我们需要把自己最想强调的信息放在最能引起读者视觉注意的地方。通常来讲，一句话的开头会或多或少地照应前文提过的信息，形成连贯；而一句话偏向结束的地方，往往是信息的着重点，我们需要把重点想要强调的信息放在这里。

　　下面这三个例子，表达的信息侧重点是不一样的：

　　　　例1：Romeo loves Juliet.（Romeo 爱的是 Juliet，不是别人）

　　　　例2：Juliet is loved by Romeo.（爱 Juliet 的不是别人，是

Romeo)

例3：Juliet is loved.（Juliet 是被爱的，不是被恨的）

下面的例子是我经常在期末考试的前一周对学生说的。不难发现，改变了信息的位置，强调的重点也有所变化。

例1：I hope you will be fully prepared and arrive on time.（强调的是 arrive on time）

例2：I hope that you will arrive on time and be fully prepared.（强调的是 be fully prepared）

我们再来看一个稍长的段落①，请大家思考横线处应该填 A 句还是 B 句。

Too often in science we operate under the principle that "to name it is to tame it," or so we think. One of the easiest mistakes, even among working scientists, is to believe that labeling something has somehow or other added to an explanation or understanding of it. Worse than that, we use it all the time when we're reac-

---

① FIRESTEIN S. The name game. [G] // BROCKMAN J. This will make you smarter. New York: Harper Perennial, 2012, 62-64.

hing, leading students to believe that a phenomenon named is a phenomenon known, and that to know a name is to know the phenomenon. _____. In biology especially we have labels for everything—molecules, anatomical parts, physiological functions, organisms, ideas, hypotheses. The nominal fallacy is the error of believing that the label carries explanatory information.

A：Nominal fallacy is what I and others called this phenomenon.
B：It is what I and others have called the nominal fallacy.

通过上下文的通读，我们知道，这里是给前文描述的现象一个抽象概念。如果填入 A 句，在强调点出现的信息是 phenomenon，但 phenomenon 显然不是我们这句话想要强调的重点。重点信息是什么？是 nominal fallacy，然而我们却得往回看，才能看到重点信息。而填入 B 句，读者在强调点的位置上看到了全句最重要的、作者最想强调的信息，读起来非常舒服，也非常节能。

以上是安排句中信息位置的一个原则：**把需要重点突出的信息放在句子的强调点上**。

我们再来看看英国科学史教授罗布艾利夫所著的《牛顿新传》的开篇几句：

Unconscious since late on the previous Saturday evening, Sir Isaac Newton died soon after 1 a.m. on Monday 20 March 1727 at the age of 84. He was attended at his passing by his physician Richard Mead, who later told the great French philosopher Voltaire that on his deathbed Newton had confessed he was a virgin. Newton was also looked after in his final hours by his half-niece Catherine and her husband John Conduitt, who had acted as a sort of personal assistant to Newton in his final years. ①

在不改变这一段落主要信息的前提下，我们把信息的位置变一变，请同学们来体会一下两个段落的区别。

Unconscious since late on the previous Saturday evening, Sir Isaac Newton died soon after 1 a.m. on Monday 20 March 1727 at the age of 84. His physician Richard Mead attend at his passing and he later told the great French philosopher Voltaire that on his deathbed Newton had confessed he was a virgin. Newton's half-niece Catherine and her husband John Conduitt also looked after him in his final hours. He had acted as a sort of personal assistant to Newton in his final years.

从读者的角度，两个段落的区别显而易见。第一个段落的三句话都以牛顿为主语，讲述了一个关于牛顿的故事：他是什么时候去世的，临终是由谁照顾的。而第二个段落，从第二个句子起，

---

① 罗布·艾利夫. 牛顿新传[M]. 万兆元,译. 北京:译林出版社,2015: 1.

由于改变了主语，信息的重点由牛顿本人转向了他的送终者。两个段落信息无异，但信息的位置影响了我们对信息重点的解读。

再举个例子。很多同学写学术文章喜欢用"Recently, there are a lot of research on…"开头。从语法的角度，这样的句型毫无问题，但读者读到最后，才能明白这段话要讲的是"谁的故事"。不如把故事的主角明显地放在主语的位置，如：

Ultraviolet (UV) photodetectors have been extensively investigated due to their great applications in missile detection and interception, flame and environment monitoring, chemical and biological sensing, UV astronomy and spectroscopy.[①]

因此，落笔写下一个句子，尤其是一个简单句时，我们需要考虑的是：这是谁的故事？读者通常期待简单句讲述的是最先出现的那个人/物的故事。**我们要把故事的主角放在主语的位置上**。

我们再来看看复合句中信息位置的选择。以前我们学习复合句，多是从语法正确的角度去看待（比如选择which，还是that）。我们学习学术写作，可以从信息的有效传达这个角度多思考。这需要我们回到复合句最朴素的定义。

复合句中，有一个主句和至少一个从句。主句意味着主导，

[①] Wang F X, Chang D M, Lu Z Q. AlGaN-based p-i-p-i-n solar-blind ultraviolet avalanche photodetectors with modulated polarization electric field［J］. International Journal of Numerical Modelling: Electronic Networks, Devices and Fields, 2020, 33(6), e2763. https://doi.org/10.1002/jnm.2763

主导意味着相对重要；从句意味着从属，从属意味着相对不重要。读者通常期待的是主句中出现的人或事，所以我们要把想强调的信息放在主句中。

以学术论文为例，什么是我们最想强调的信息呢？通常来讲是研究的发现、意义和价值。这就需要我们想清楚自己的贡献。比如，我在方法上有贡献吗？我提出了一个新方法？还是改进了别人的方法？

如果我们提出了一个新方法解决了一个老问题，可以把方法放在主句的位置，比如：

This paper proposed an innovative method, which…

如果我们用了一个老方法解决了一个新问题，但这个方法也不是原封不动地照搬别人，而是有所改进，我们可以把方法通过分词短语（或从句）呈现出来，淡化方法的分量，而把新问题放在主句的位置。

This paper, using a method adapted from ** (year), aims to investigate…

事实上，除了那些和研究的发现、意义、价值直接相关的句子，我们对每一个表达了复杂意思的句子，在落笔之前都要琢磨信息的主次。我曾在一篇论文的初稿里写了下面这个句子：

The textbook consists of ten chapters, with the first five chapters focusing on critical reading skills and source-based writing skills.

从语法的角度,这句话挑不出什么毛病。修改时,我问自己:这句话想突出的是"这本教材包括十章"吗?显然不是。于是,我调整了一下句子的结构,把这句话真正的信息重点凸显了出来。

Of the textbook's ten chapters, the first five chapters focused on critical reading skills and source-based writing skills.

再来看一个学生论文中的例子。

Several researchers believe that video learning does little help to study. For example, after receiving introduction videos before every lecture, students in Park University were less likely to quit the course or fail, though they did not get better average scores (Hsin and Cigas, 2013). Similarly, Dong and Hong's (2018) research conducted on Chinese students claimed that internet video media made little impact on school scores.

这个段落中,作者引用了两项研究,来证明"视频学习对学生帮助不大"的观点。其中第一个引用的信息安排有些问题。作者将"less likely to quit the course or fail"放在主句的位置,强调了这部分的信息,而这个信息却不能作为"对学生帮助不大"的证据。更为合理的安排是将主句和从句中的信息互换,让"they did not get better average scores"在句中凸显出来。

由上面几个例子可见,在选词相同的情况下,读者感受到的信息重点,是由句子结构和词语所在的位置决定的。

以上我们讲了简单句和复合句中,如何合理安排信息的位置。下面我们重点关注一类词——动词,看看这类词在句中的位置。

《结构感》① 一书的作者戈彭教授把句子主语和谓语动词的依存关系比作两只鞋的关系。在主语(一只鞋)出现后,等待谓语动词出现,就好比等待另一只鞋出现。因此,**在一句话的语法主语出现(也就是明晰了这是关于"谁"的故事)后,读者通常会期待一个谓语动词紧跟其后**。

正因如此,句子主语和谓语动词之间出现的信息都可被看作是次要的干扰信息。心中期待动词的来临,我们往往会低声快速地阅读主语之后、动词之前的部分。而如果这部分信息恰好是作者最想强调的,最想引起读者注意的,读者就极易被不合理的句子结构误导,到了句末发现略过了重要信息,回头重读,这是对能量的消耗。一起来看下面的例子。

In this study, students' performance assessed at different periods of time are compared.

---

① GOPEN G D. The sense of structure: Writing from the reader's perspective [M]. London: Pearson Education Inc, 2004:32.

上句中，句子的主语是 the care，随后是一个长长的后置定语，需要一直读到最后，才能看到句子的谓语（are compared）。读者为了尽早知晓句子的谓语，容易忽略掉主语和谓语之间的重要信息。试与下句比较：

> The study compared students' performance assessed at different periods of time.

可以看到，经过结构调整，句子的核心意义没有改变，但主语和谓语的连接却更为紧密了，作者要强调的重要信息也落在了句子的强调点上。大家不妨再读一下这两个句子，从读者的角度，体会一下哪句话当中的信息更容易处理。

肯定有同学会问，学术语篇中不是鼓励使用被动句吗？这么说来，是要把被动句都改成主动句？

被动句在学术文章中的确是很常见的。我们使用被动句，是为了淡化人的因素对研究的影响。但使用被动句，和主谓语之间的紧密连接这一点并不冲突。我们看下面一个段落[①]。这个段落来自一篇学术论文的方法部分。

Participants were 67 students (33 male, 33 female, 1 unknown)

---

① MUELLER P A, OPPENHEIMER D M. The pen is mightier than the keyboard: Advantages of longhand over laptop note taking [J]. Psychological Science, 2014, 25(6): 1159-1168.

from the Princeton University subject pool. Two participants were excluded, 1 because he had seen the lecture serving as the stimulus prior to participation, and 1 because of a data-recording error.

We selected five TED Talks (https://www.ted.com/talks) for length (slightly over 15 min) and to cover topics that would be interesting but not common knowledge. 2 Laptops had full-size (11-in. × 4-in.) keyboards and were disconnected from the Internet.

Students generally participated 2 at a time, though some completed the study alone. The room was preset with either laptops or notebooks, according to condition. Lectures were projected onto a screen at the front of the room. Participants were instructed to use their normal classroom note-taking strategy, because experimenters were interested in how information was actually recorded in class lectures. The experimenter left the room while the lecture played.

Next, participants were taken to a lab; they completed two 5-min distractor tasks and engaged in a taxing working memory task (viz., a reading span task; Unsworth, Heitz, Schrock, & Engle, 2005). At this point, approximately 30 min had elapsed since the end of the lecture. Finally, participants responded to both factual-recall questions (e.g., "Approximately how many years ago did the Indus civilization exist?") and conceptual-application questions (e.g., "How do Japan and Sweden differ in their approaches to equality within their societies?") about the lecture and completed demographic measures.

The first author scored all responses blind to condition. An independent rater, blind to the purpose of the study and condition, also scored all open-ended questions. Initial interrater reliability was good (α = .89); <u>score disputes between raters were resolved</u> by discussion. <u>Longhand notes were transcribed</u> into text files.

以上八个画线的句子都是被动句，但我们看到主谓语之间的联系是比较紧密的。再回到我们之前的那个例子。如果我们想保留被动句式，又想让主谓语之间的联系紧密的话，不妨把谓语部分提前：

In this study, also compared is students' performance assessed at different periods of time.

这一讲，我们从句子类型和句中信息的安排两个方面探讨了句子的写作和锤炼。炼句的最终目的是减少读者的能量损耗，保持他们的阅读兴致，帮助他们最快速有效地捕捉到作者想要传达的信息。

最后回到本讲开头的那个问题：下一个句子怎么写？

我想我们不必要求自己落笔形成的就是一个方方面面都堪称完美的句子。我们需要先写出一个句子，然后再去追求那"唯一的句子"。

本讲练习

1. 以下选句来自学生《影响大学生信任水平的因素》的研究论文。这篇论文研究了大学生的信任水平和其性别、专业、内/外向性格倾向的关联。这篇文章存在过度使用定语从句的倾向。请你重写画线的部分,使该部分的表意更清晰,信息重点更突出。

(1) Trust is the belief that somebody or something is good, sincere, honest and so on (McLeod, 2011). It deeply influences how an individual reacts to numerous situations in his/her life, thus affecting his/her development in various aspects. It's also a prevalent point of view that a trust crisis exists in today's society, which may help to explain why studying people's trust tendency becomes increasingly important.

(2) Wang et al. (2005) summarized 6 factors influencing trust among people, which are social similarity, degree of knowing other people, personal perspective on his/her own personality, social status, social culture background and law.

(3) Barbara (1985) found that the initial trust of subjects can be strongly affected by both first impressions and the source's reliability, but first impressions are found to have an even

stronger effect after the analysis of subjects' overall trusting behavior. This result points out the importance of the "lead-in process", which means the ways in which the subjects participate in or are led into trust tendency experiments are quite important.

(4) In the questionnaire, respondents were given seventeen statements describing real situations that were related to trust. The questionnaire included 2 additional questions which were deliberately designed to be quite similar to two previous questions. We used the answers of them to check if the questionnaire had been finished earnestly.

(5) According to the X^2 test which was performed to assess the relevance between gender and trust propensity; majors and trust propensity; personality (introvert or extrovert) and trust propensity, we found that gender and college students' trust tendency showed obvious relativity ($K^2=3.922$, $P>0.95$), but the relevance between major and trust propensity and personality and trust tendency was not so distinct ($K^2=0.920$, $P<0.75$; $K^2=0.268$, $P<0.5$).

2. 以下选句来自学生《重力和磁力对黏菌的影响》的研究论文。这篇论文存在过度使用"there be"句型的倾向。请你重写下面的几个句子，让句子的主语凸显出来。

(1) There were researches in the slime mold's area extension on plain plates, but investigation in their extension on angled plates remained blank.

(2) After comprehensive view of these papers, though many excellent conclusions have been drawn by others, there are still some unsolved problems left.

(3) Our analyses revealed that the slime mold has the "gravitropic responses", but there is no solid evidence shown that the slime mold's growth is highly affected to magneticenvironment.

(4) Although we reached the results through experiments, there were limitations awaiting our effort to cover, which contains that controlled conditions are not strict enough and sample size is not big enough.

(5) Though the growing speed was influenced, there was little impact on the direction that the slime mold chose.

3. 以下选句均来自学生论文的讨论部分，介绍了各自研究的不足之处。请你将句中标志研究不足的部分画线，并思考研究不足在哪几个句子中凸显出来了，在哪几个句子中被作者有效地弱化了。

(1) Still, the study has a few limitations and challenges that the future research should consider.

(2) Although the result has shown the superiority of M/M/c queuing form based on the statistic collected from UCAS, we fail to give the proof under common conditions.

(3) Although our experimental results did not meet the expectations, they reveal what should be paid attention to in material selection, and provide guidance for the subsequent related experiments.

(4) Notably, despite that our results are less than satisfactory compared with our prediction, we are the first to carry out research on the relationship between music preferences and the mastering of instruments within our range of knowledge.

(5) Although there are some significant discoveries shown this study, there are still several limitations.

第六讲　用　词

这一讲，我们谈谈学术写作中的用词。学术写作中的用词应是：准确、简洁、有活力。

准确是基础要求。准确就是作者想表达的意思和实际表达出来的意思是一致的，读者不会对表达出来的意思产生误解；简洁是进阶要求。简洁就是无冗余的信息，每一个词都有其作用和分量，不可减省；有活力是高阶要求。学术写作通常承载了有活力的思想，我们应该把有活力的思想用有活力的语言表达出来。

（一）准确

美国语言学家肯尼斯·派克说："语言是一个工具。它足以在一个特定的情景下呈现不同的准确程度。"[①] 我们日常的生活情境往往对说话的准确性不作很高的要求。试想男孩对一个他喜欢的女孩说："我喜欢你。你喜欢我吗？"他更有可能得到的回答是"我喜欢你"，"我不喜欢你"，还是"你觉得呢""我喜欢大海"呢？

---

① PIKE K L. With heart and mind: A personal synthesis of scholarship and devotion [M]. Michigan: William B. Eerdmans Publishing Company, 1962: 40.

聚焦到写作上，不同类型的写作往往对准确性有不同的要求。对一部好的文学作品，我们常说："一千个读者，就有一千个哈姆雷特。"创意写作能给读者留下丰富的想象和解读的空间；而对于学术写作，准确是前提。任何模糊、有歧义的表达都是不准确的体现，会干扰读者快速有效地理解科学事实。

讲一个和用语"准确"有关的写作经历。一次，我在设计一个七级量表时，对七个选项的表述如下：1 = definitely not plagiarized，2 = probably not plagiarized，3 = likely not plagiarized，4 = unsure，5 = likely to be plagiarized，6 = probably plagiarized，7 = definitely plagiarized。

投稿后审稿人回复，在他/她的语感里面，likely 的可能性是要大于 probably 的。我上网搜索了表可能性的词，其间意外地看到了一张 2015 年"信息之美"的获奖作品。

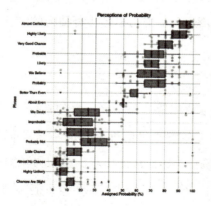

图 6-1　关于可能性的认知①

---

① Data Visualization Society. Information is beautiful awards [EB/OL]. [2022-11-02] https://www.informationisbeautifulawards.com/showcase/818-perceptions-of-probability

从这张图来看，probably 和 likely 所表达的可能性高低难以达成定论。后来，我请教了几个外教同事。在他们的建议下，我把 2 和 6 的表述分别改为 more than likely not plagiarized 和 more than likely to be plagiarized，这样的修改是在无法完全准确的地方找到了相对准确的可能性。

除了斟酌用词、体察词语间的细微差异，准确表意也需要考虑词语的位置。副词的位置最能体现学术语言对准确的要求。请大家先看下面这个段落，标示出其中的所有副词，观察它们的位置。

The vision community has rapidly improved object detection and semantic segmentation results over a short period of time. In large part, these advances have been driven by powerful baseline systems, such as the Fast/Faster R-CNN and Fully Convolutional Network (FCN) frameworks for object detection and semantic segmentation, respectively. These methods are conceptually intuitive and offer flexibility and robustness, together with fast training and inference time. Our goal in this work is to develop a comparably enabling framework for instance segmentation.[1]

这个段落中出现的副词，依次是 rapidly, respectively, conceptu-

---

[1] HE K, GKIOXARI G, DOLLÁR P, et al. Mask R-CNN [C]. Proceedings of the IEEE International Conference on Computer Vision, 2017, 2980-2988.

ally, comparably。可以看到，rapidly, conceptually, comparably 出现的位置都是句中（可能不同于我们印象中副词应该出现的位置）。这些副词和 improve, intuitive, enabling 紧密相连，修饰关系非常清晰。唯一出现在结尾的副词是 respectively。该句如果去掉 respectively 一词，有的读者可能会认为在目标检测（object detection）和语义切分（semantic segmentation）方面使用的都是全卷积网络框架（Fully Convolutional Network frameworks），而在句末补上 respectively 一词，消除了可能的歧义，表意十分准确。

下面，我们通过一些语言实例，看看如何改进语义模糊和容易引起歧义的句子。

（1）合理使用逻辑连接词，清楚地表明信息之间的关系。

先举个汉语的例子。2022 年 3 月东航一架从云南飞往广州的客机失事。随后的几天，各种新闻铺天盖地。我看到一则新闻的标题这样写道：

失事客机飞行员健康状况良好

这个标题很可能让人误以为飞行员还活着。稍加分析不难发现，问题出现在"失事客机"这里。从汉语的语感上，"失事客机"是"飞行员"的定语，是这个标题中似乎不重要的信息。其实作者想表达的意思是，客机失事前，飞行员健康状况良好。把"失事"和"客机"的位置互换，并在"客机失事"后加上

"前"，可能有的歧义就消解了。

再来看一个英文的例子。

例：Students' English proficiency level in the three groups was comparable in the in-house placement test.

在这句话中，作者想要传达的意思是：从入学考试成绩得知，三组学生的英语水平具有可比性。但这句话表述的不准确，读者可能会把这句话解读为：各组学生参加入学考试时英语水平相当。这和作者想要表达的意思很不一致了。

修改后：Students' English proficiency level was comparable as measured by the in-house placement test.

加入 as measured by...后，句中信息之间的关系明朗了，表意也准确了。

（2）选择合理的时态（或时间词），清楚地表明事件的先后次序。

例：Shortly after being instructed in the EAP unit focusing on source attribution, students who consented to participate in the study were administered a questionnaire designed by the researcher.

熟悉教学研究的读者不难理顺本句提到主要事件的先后次序。但由于该句中，主句和从句都使用了一般过去时，学生"上课""做问卷""同意参与实验"几件事的先后顺序不够清晰，容易引起一般读者的困扰。为了表意准确，我们可以通过时态的选择，清楚地表明事件的先后次序。

修改后：Shortly after being instructed in the EAP unit focusing on source attribution, students who had consented to participate in the study were administered a questionnaire designed by the researcher.

如用中文表达这句话的意思，在"同意"一词之前加上"先前"是很有必要的：学生们刚上完关于文献征引的教学单元，那些先前同意参加研究的学生完成了研究者设计的一份问卷。

例：Hu and Lei's (2012) questionnaire on referencing knowledge, which contains seven scenarios with typical examples of textual plagiarism found in Anglo-American academia, was then used to promote critical thinking in the discussion.

定冠词 the+名词通常指代前文提过的事物，因此上例中的 the discussion 可能会引起读者的困惑（上文没有出现过 discussion）。加上时间词，可清晰地呈现分发问卷和讨论的先后顺序。

修改后：Hu and Lei's (2012) questionnaire on referencing knowledge, which contains seven scenarios with typical examples of textual plagiarism found in Anglo-American academia, was then used to promote critical thinking in the ensuing discussion.

(3) 慎用语义模糊的词。

例：In debating the reasons students gave to support their stance, students were drawn to a deeper level of evaluation involving aspects such as originality, creativity, imitation, humor/sarcasm, innovation, etc.

"等等"在口语和非学术文体中常能见到。不过，"等等"给读者留下了想象的空间，可能会引起读者不同的解读。因此，这一类词在学术语境下并不常用。在 such as, including 这样的小词后，我们通常只列出若干项目，以句号结尾，不加"等等"。

修改后：In debating the reasons students gave to support their stance, students were drawn to deeper level of evaluation involving aspects such as originality, creativity, imitation, humor/sarcasm, and innovation.

例：The findings of our study are consistent with those of Liu

(2020) and Yang et al. (2013), which found that the undergraduate tutorial system is beneficial to help students quickly adapt to university life.

此处which指的是Yang et al. (2013)的研究发现，还是Liu (2020)和Yang et al. (2013)的共同发现？Which作为非限定性定语从句的引导词，常常会出现指代模糊的现象。为了表意准确，我们可以用两句话来表述。

修改后：The findings of our study are consistent with those of Liu (2020) and Yang et al. (2013). Both studies found that the undergraduate tutorial system is beneficial to help students quickly adapt to university life.

（二）简洁

我们首先要明确：简洁是准确基础上的简洁。换言之，简洁不能以牺牲准确为代价。

如何做到简洁呢？罗伊·克拉克教授在《写作工具》这本书里写道："先裁剪大的枝干，再抖落掉枯枝败叶。"① 可见，我们首先要删去和文章整体的论证逻辑不相容的段落，也就是大的枝干。

---

① CLARK R P. Writing tools: 55 essential strategies for every writer [M]. New York: Little, Brown Spark, 2008: 51.

之后，我们可以仔细地雕琢词句，抖落文中的枯枝败叶。抖落字词层面冗余的信息，需要些精细的功夫。威廉·津瑟教授在《写作法宝：非虚构写作指南》一书中将这个功夫描述为："剥离每一句话中的杂物，只留存其最洁净的部分。"①

威廉·斯特伦克在《风格的要素》② 也有关于"简洁"的一段精彩的论述。董桥在《老教授的那本小册子》中将其翻译如下：

> 铿然有力之文必简洁。一句之中无赘字，一段之中无赘句，犹如丹青无冗枝，机器无废件。此说不求作者下笔句句精短，摒弃细节，概而述之；但求字字有着落耳。③

要留下每句话中"最洁净"的部分，给句子"瘦身"，我们不妨问自己几个问题：

1. 句中某个部分的意义是不是在其他部分已有体现？
2. 句中某些词是不是没有给该句话增添实质性的信息？
3. 句中某个部分能否在不改变意义的前提下，用更简洁的形式表达？

---

① Zinsser W. On writing well: The classic guide to writing nonfiction [M]. New York: Harper Perennial, 2016: 6.
② STRUNK W, WHITE E B, KALMAN M. The elements of style [M]. New York: Penguin Group, 2007: 39.
③ 董桥. 品味历程[M]. 北京：生活.读书.新知三联书店，2002: 237. 原文为：Vigorous writing is concise. A sentence should contain no unnecessary words, a paragraph no unnecessary sentences, for the same reason that a drawing should have no unnecessary lines and a machine no unnecessary parts. This requires not that the writer make all his sentences short, or that he avoid all detail and treat his subjects only in outline, but that every word tell.

如果句子某个部分的意义在其他部分已有体现，需要果断删掉冗余，避免重复。如"The definition of charismatic leaders is not clearly defined."一句中，definition 和 defined 的意义有重复。这句话可以改为"The definition of charismatic leader is not clear."或者"The concept of charismatic leaders is not clearly defined."。

下面句子中的画线部分也都属于冗余词：

(1) After Cycle 1, some obvious progress was noted in students' <u>own</u> writing.

(2) Students readthe 1979 article on <u>the subject of</u> "a new drug for malaria" published in China Reconstructs and noted how the scientist who contributed to the discovery was credited.

(3) The development of satellite <u>earth</u> terrestrial observation technology in the past several decades has made it possible to realize globally continuous monitoring and inversion of physical parameters of snow/ice.

(4) Dynamism and velocity are <u>typical</u> characteristics of this species.

(5) We have made an *advance* plan for the project.

(6) Another *possible* approach is to calculate P before Q.

(7) Chemical reactions between organic materials and pigments lead to discoloration *phenomena*.

(8) Our research *activity* consists of x and y.

(9) Similarly, Dong and Hong's (2018) research *conducted* on Chinese students claimed that internet video media made little impact on school scores.

(10) The results *obtained* highlight that X＝Y.

切忌频繁使用不能给文章增添实质内容的短语和小句。如下例中画线的部分：

(1) *It should be noted here* each study cycle had a different class; there was no overlap in students between cycles. An equal number of students (n＝32) were involved in each cycle.

(2) *It is possible to say* since the critical-pragmatic approach to source-attribution instruction worked well in practice in this classroom setting, instruction of other aspects of academic literacy skills might benefit from similar circumstances.

和这类短语和小句功能相似的还包括"It should be pointed out that…""It is noteworthy that…""It is significant that…""I might add that…",这类表达偶尔出现,能起到一定的修辞效果,但如果经常使用,会适得其反。试想一篇文章满篇儿都是"非常重要",读者在某处看到"重要"一词时,反而会觉得不重要了。

表达意义相似的两个句子,选用形式上更为简洁的。试比较下面几组句子:

修改前:Students who obtained a score below 70 were required to take this course.

修改后:Students who scored below 70 were required to take this course.

修改前:A questionnaire on referencing knowledge from Hu and Lei (2012) was used in the study.

修改后:Hu and Lei's (2012) questionnaire on referencing knowledge was used in the study.

修改前:The textbook used in the course, compiled by a team of actively teaching faculty members at the same university, was designed and targeted at students of low-to-intermediate level English proficiency.

修改后:The course textbook, compiled by a team of actively teaching faculty members at the same university, was designed and targeted at students of low-to-intermediate level English proficiency.

相比于删掉冗余词和不能给文章增加实质内容的短语和小句，这一点最困难，也是自我校正时很难发觉的。如第一组例子涉及的是词性问题，而第二、三两组例子是所属关系和介词的问题。相较而言，第二、三两组例子有一些共性，多揣摩和体会的话能收到举一反三的成效；而词的层面的简洁，则要靠日积月累了。

（三）有活力

学术写作中，如果准确是底线、简洁是良心，那有活力就是读者的福音了。

不知道大家平日阅读时有没有这样的体验：明明对一篇文章研究的内容很感兴趣，但就是读不下去，觉得文章死气沉沉的。学术思想充满生机与活力，我们如何能让承载学术思想的语言也充满生机与活力？

试想，一个风和日丽的天儿，一艘海上航行的货船沉没了，可能的原因是什么？如果我们不考虑撞上冰山这样的外因，一个很可能的原因是发动机出了故障，失灵了。一个句子的发动机是什么？是谓语动词。谓语动词，能给一个句子注入能量。如果一个句子读来毫无活力，多半是谓语动词的问题。来看两个例子：

例1：We make a comparison between A and B.

例2：The recruitment of new team members was conducted via email campaigns.

写作时，我们有时会把最主要的动作包裹在名词中。例1的"做比较"（make a comparison）中，谓语动词"做"（make）没有为这个短语增添额外的信息，而主要动作"比较"是通过名词comparison表达的；例2的谓语动词是一个be动词，而主要动作"招募"也是通过名词recruitment表达的。把包裹在名词中的动词释放出来，句子的活力就大大地增强了。以上两句可修改为：

例1：We compare between A and B./A and B are compared.

例2：We recruited new team members via email campaigns. / New team members were recruited via email campaigns.

可见，适当地释放动词是增加句子活力的有效途径，就像打篮球时，传球直接、干脆，不拖泥带水，这样才最有力量。

以上我们谈的是学术写作中用词的一般原则（准确、简洁、有活力）。下面，我们来谈谈冠词、人称代词、连词这三类小词的使用。

（一）冠词

有人说，看看冠词的使用大概就能判断出文章是出自母语者还是非母语者了，可见冠词的准确使用并不容易。我们不需要追求冠词使用的万无一失，因为偶尔的失误可能并不影响理解。但英语的冠词就像中文的"的""地""得"，在文章中无处不在，因此我们还是要避免一些规律性的错误。我总结了同学们论文中冠词的使用，发现不当的使用有下面几类。

(1) 该使用零冠词而使用了定冠词/不定冠词

例 1：Nevertheless, the active video learning, referring to searching videos to learn instead of receiving ones from teachers, is still not thoroughly investigated.

例 1 中 active video learning 是一个作者在文章开头界定的核心概念，不需使用定冠词/不定冠词修饰。

修改后：Nevertheless, active video learning, referring to searching videos to learn instead of receiving ones from teachers, is still not thoroughly investigated.

（2）该使用不定冠词/定冠词而使用了零冠词（冠词丢失）

例 2：For the necessity of video learning, more than half of respondents believe that online video learning helps but is not the main source for acquiring knowledge.

例 2 来自文章的结果部分：超过一半的 respondents 认为在线视频虽然有用，但不是获取知识的主要来源。由于 respondents 的情况在前文已有介绍，这里应在 respondents 前面加上定冠词 the，特指本项研究的 respondents。

修改后：For the necessity of video learning, more than half of <u>the</u> respondents believe that online video learning helps but is not the main source for acquiring knowledge.

（3）该使用不定冠词而使用了定冠词

例 3：When traveling indoors, one possible situation they may face is to either climb stairs or take the elevator.

例 4：Data analysis revealed that the time of the day is an influential factor. And the day of the week seems to be irrelevant.

以上两句来自学生《哪个更快：使用电梯还是爬楼梯?》的论文。例 3 来自研究的背景，描述了人们常有的困境；例 4 来自研究发现，一天的不同时间是重要的影响因素，而一周的哪一天影响甚微。例 3 中的"坐电梯"，例 4 中的"一天""一周"都是普遍意义上的，不需要特指。这两句话可修改为：

例 3：When traveling indoors, one possible situation students may face is to either climb stairs or take <u>an</u> elevator.

例 4：Data analysis revealed that the time of <u>a</u> day is an influential factor. And the day of <u>a</u> week seems to be irrelevant.

（二）人称代词

每一轮开设学术写作课，都有同学提到第一人称代词的困扰："老师，学术论文中是不是不能用'I''We'这样的第一人称代词啊？"

我建议同学们在目标期刊里下载几篇文章，搜索 I 和 We。如果第一人称代词在文章中确有使用，仔细观察它们通常在哪些部分、哪些语境下使用。

下面，我们以《科学》杂志上一篇文章①的引言为例说明人称代词的使用。

---

① TIAN Z, ZHAO H, PETER K T, et al. A ubiquitous tire rubber-derived chemical induces acute mortality in coho salmon [J]. Science, 2020, doi:10.1126/science.abd6951

Humans discharge tens of thousands of chemicals and related transformation products to water[1], most of which remain unidentified and lack rigorous toxicity information[2]. Efforts to identify and mitigate high risk chemical toxicants are typically reactionary, occur long after their use becomes habitual[3], and are frequently stymied by mixture complexity. Societal management of inadvertent, yet widespread, chemical pollution is therefore costly, challenging, and often ineffective.

The pervasive biological degradation of contaminated waters near urban areas (i.e., "urban stream syndrome")[4] is exemplified by an acute mortality phenomenon affecting Pacific Northwest coho salmon (Oncorhynchus kisutch) for decades[5-9]. "Urban runoff mortality syndrome" (URMS) occurs annually among adult coho salmon returning to spawn in freshwaters where concurrent stormwater exposure causes rapid mortality. In the most urbanized watersheds with extensive impervious surfaces, 40-90% of returning salmon may die before spawning[9]. This mortality threatens salmonid species conservation across ~40% of Puget Sound land area despite costly societal investments in physical habitat restoration that may have inadvertently created ecological traps due to episodic toxic water pollution[9]. Although URMS has been linked to degraded water quality, urbanization, and high traffic intensity[9],

第六讲 用 词 ▌ 149

one or more causal toxicants have remained unidentified. Spurred by these compelling observations and mindful of the many other insidious sublethal stormwater impact, we have worked to characterize URMS water quality[10-11].

Previously, we reported that URMS-associated waters had similar chemical compositions relative to roadway runoff and tire tread wear particle (TWP) leachates, providing an opening clue in our toxicant search[10]. Here, we applied hybrid toxicity identification evaluation and effect-directed analysis to screen TWP leachate for its potential to induce mortality (a phenotypic anchor) in juvenile coho salmon as an experimental proxy for adult coho[6]. Using structural identification via ultrahigh performance liquid chromatography-high resolution tandem mass spectrometry (UPLC-HRMS/MS) and nuclear magnetic resonance (NMR), we discovered that an antioxidant-derived chemical was the primary causal toxicant. Retrospective analysis of runoff and receiving waters indicated that detected environmental concentrations of this toxicant often exceeded acute mortality thresholds for coho during URMS events in the field and across the U.S. West Coast.

这一部分共 13 句话，其中连续 4 句都出现了 we，但作为读者，我们却没有觉得作者一直在强调自己。为什么？因为作者对

we 的处理很有技巧。第 9 句，作者用过去分词引导状语从句，讲自己之前，认可了别人的贡献（these compelling observations）和别人对自己的启发（Spurred by…）；第 10 句，在 we 之前，作者使用时间状语 previously，说明自己的研究并非一蹴而就，而是基于过去的积累；第 11 句，作者在 we 之前，使用了 here，相当于 in this study，把读者的注意力指向研究本身，而不是研究者上；第 12 句，作者使用现在分词（using）引导状语从句，讲自己的发现之前，先介绍采用的方法。

可见，当我们确要使用 I 或 We 的时候，首先一定要确保它们用在了刀刃上，也就是用在了能体现我们的创新和贡献之处。此外，使用 I 或 We 时，可以将它们适当挪后，避免频繁地在句首使用 I 或 We。

（三）连词

连词看上去平淡无奇，但用得合适着实不易。同学们论文中的连词误用，主要有以下两类。

（1）有些词没有连词的用法，却误作连词使用

　　例 1：This teaching system was traced back to the 14th century at Oxford University and Cambridge University, then imitated by many high-level universities, such as Harvard University.

此例中，then 是个副词，并没有连词的用法。我们需要为这句话增加连词。

修改后：This teaching system was traced back to the 14th century at Oxford University and Cambridge University and was later imitated by many high-level universities, such as Harvard University.

（2）并列连词（如 and, but, or, nor）在学术书面语中，通常不用在句首

并列连词（coordinating conjunctions）通常是用来连接词、短语、小句的。我们在写一个句子时，要思考清楚其与上一句话的联系，不能习惯性地使用并列连词开头。

例1：When asked for the reasons why they seldom communicate with their tutors, students reported the main reasons are heavy academic load and busy schedule (more than three out of four), and being scared to contact their tutors (more than three out of five). And these two reasons reflect two kinds of pressure, schoolwork pressure, and psychological pressure.

此例中，前句呈现了学生很少与导师沟通的两个原因。后句中，作者将两个原因归结为两方面的压力。其中的 these two reasons 与前句衔接自然，并列连词 and 在此处是多余的。

需要说明的是，并列连词不用在句首并不是绝对的。当后句比照前句，有意追求某些表达效果（如强调、对比）时，可以使用并列连词（如下面两例），但不建议过度使用。

例 2：Now there's no doubt that physicists themselves would be the first ones to recognize the value of experimentalists; for instance, Anderson, Davis, and Kendall-Friedman-Taylor trio were all recognized by Nobel Prizes. But their recognition in the public mind ranges from vague to non-existence.（前两句讲"学界认可实验物理学家的贡献"，末句讲"公众对实验物理学家贡献的认可甚微"，句首 But 凸显了差异。）

例 3：An even more pointed and roaring tribute to experiment came from the utter self-assured king of experimental physics, Ernest Rutherford. His opinion of theoreticians was that "they play games with symbols, but we turn out the real facts of Nature". And he is said to have admonished the capable students working under his tutelage — nine of them won Nobel Prizes — to not "let me catch anyone talking about the Universe".（前两句讲了 Rutherford 对实验的高度认可，并引用了他的一句话佐证这一点。到这里我们已经能感到 Rutherford 满满的自信了。但作者在此基础上又添一例，句首 And 进一步强调了 Rutherford 对实验的重视。）

这一讲我们讲了学术写作中用词的基本原则和几类小词的用法，不妨拿起你手头的一篇文章，试试修改一段。

本讲练习

1. 下面的选段来自学生题为"The use of iPad among college students"论文的讨论部分。请你先通读这个部分,然后完成段落后面的几个练习。

Discussion

The purpose of this study was to investigate how modern university students' study was affected by iPads. The results show that respondents mainly benefited from note-taking apps and video apps that best meet university students' daily needs respectively for taking notes and learning courses.

Specifically, for one thing, useful notetaking apps on iPad are advantageous platforms for screen noting where information can be well-kept and easy to move and sort through. Among the results, *Notability* and *Goodnotes* were most respondents' top choices. Compared with hand-written notes, *Notability* notes provide limitless spaces for drafting and recording fleeting inspirations, while *Goodnotes* with more than 20 notebook styles available can satisfy individual needs for note typography and its diverse marking colors facilitate personal note-highlighting. We also concluded through our survey that it is convenient to actually write by hand on the screen with Apple Pencil and tailor useful knowledge points from PDF files to digital "handwritten" notes. For another, video apps such as *Bilibili* and *MOOK* provide a wealth of free teaching and learning resources to students who miss important points in class. 9% of our respondents claimed their customization of watching online courses to self-study missed points or skills that are not taught in school.

Although some of our respondents expressed that due to the easy access to entertainment apps on iPads, they were more susceptible to be distracted from concentrating on learning, there are a great number of them reporting that iPad has a positive impact on cognitive skills of attention, assisting them to be more engaged in class and sustain concentration for longer time. Therefore, comparing the benefits with the defects of iPad learning, we consider the advantages outweigh the disadvantages. If there are practical measures to reduce or prevent the effect of the distraction, like the apps which are able to manage the using time of iPads, the benefits of utilizing iPad for study will be amplified.

1.1 请画出下面句子中表意不够准确的地方，思考如何使表意更为准确。

(1) Notability and Goodnotes were most respondents' top choices.

(2) 9% of our respondents claimed their customization of watching online courses to self-study missed points or skills that are not taught in school.

1.2 请用横线画掉下面句子中的冗余部分，并重写整个句子。

(1) The purpose of this study was to investigate how modern university students' study was affected by iPads.

(2) Specifically, for one thing, useful notetaking apps on iPad are advantageous platforms for screen noting where information can be well-kept and easy to move and sort through.

(3) Compared with hand-written notes, *Notability* notes provide limitless spaces for drafting and recording fleeting inspirations, while *Goodnotes* with more than 20 notebook styles available can satisfy individual needs for note typography and its diverse marking colors facilitate personal note-highlighting.

1.3 请修改下面的句子，使其更为简洁、有活力。

（1）The results show that participants mainly benefited from note-taking apps and video apps that best meet university students' daily needs respectively for taking notes and learning courses.

（2）We also concluded through our survey that it is convenient to actually write by hand on the screen with Apple Pencil and tailor useful knowledge points from PDF files to digital "handwritten" notes.

（3）Although some of our participants expressed that due to the easy access to entertainment apps on iPads, they were more susceptible to be distracted from concentrating on learning, there are a great number of them reporting that iPad has a positive impact on cognitive skills of attention, assisting them to be more engaged in class and sustain concentration for longer time.

（4）If there are practical measures to reduce or prevent the effect of the distraction, like the apps which are able to manage the using time of iPads, the benefits of utilizing iPad for study will be amplified.

2. 请你根据本讲提到的用词的基本原则（准确、简洁、有活力），修改自己论文中的五个句子。

第七讲　征　引

这一讲我们谈谈学术写作中的征引。

柯林·内维尔给了"征引"如下定义：

Referencing is the practice of acknowledging in your own writing the intellectual work of others; work that has been presented in some way into the public domain. ①

这个定义中有三个关键词：认可（acknowledging）、智力工作（intellectual work）和公共领域（public domain）。可见，征引就是对那些在公共领域的，凝结了他人智力劳动的工作，给予承认：这不是我的，这是别人的。

征引是学术写作主要特征之一。我们拿起一篇论文，即便不懂专业内容，从头到尾快速地翻一遍，也不难看到标志着文内征引的括号（或角标），以及文后长长的参考文献。虽然文献征引给

---

① NEVILLE C. The complete guide to referencing and avoiding plagiarism [M]. Berkshire: Open University Press, 2007: 1.

我们的印象可能是众多的规范和技术细节，但征引文献的理据应是学习与思考的出发点。

我们为什么在学术写作中征引文献？"避免剽窃"可能是大家最容易想到的答案。通过征引，明确区分自己和他人的观点，避免将他人的思想和语言视为己出。

英文中剽窃（plagiarism）一词起源于拉丁文 plagium，最初指"绑架了小孩或奴隶"，到了 17 世纪逐渐发展出"偷窃他人的文字"之意①，这已经很接近我们现代学术意义上的剽窃了。据《辞源》②记载，早在 8 世纪，唐代大文豪柳宗元（773—819）就用过"剽窃"一词，针砭当时的文风。

无论西方还是中国，对待剽窃的态度都是否定的。如一位曾在 17 世纪来华的意大利传教士高一志曾用不能酿蜂蜜的"乌峰"、仿效他人的"猴子"比喻"不能自造""袭取他士所作"的学人；再如《颜氏家训》中颜之推警示儿孙剽窃是窃人之美，是鬼神要惩罚的恶行。

> 乌峰不自酿蜜，而惟窃蜂蜜；学士不能自作而袭取他士所作者，乌峰之类也。……猴无业于己，以学人为业，止取人笑而已。人有不能自造，以效他人而取讥者，猴也。③

---

① MALLON T. Stolen words: Forays into the origin and ravages of plagiarism [M]. New York: Penguin, 1989.

② 何九盈，王宁，董琨. 辞源 [G]. 北京：商务印书馆，2019: 270.

③ 周振鹤（主编），姚大勇等（校点）. 明清之际西方传教士汉籍丛刊. 第一辑（2）：七克，譬学（外三种）[G]. 南京：凤凰出版社，2013: 548-549.

> 用其言，弃其身，古人所耻，凡有一言一行，取于人者，皆显称之，不可窃人之美，以为己力，虽轻虽贱者，必归功焉。窃人之财，刑辟之所处；窃人之美，鬼神之所责。①

除了"避免剽窃"，我们还可以从正面思考征引的意义。首先，征引文献可以方便读者。读者按图索骥找到原文，可以在短时间内获取大量相关的文献。而在文献又带来的新文献中，读者或能发现对自身研究更有价值的内容。

其次，征引文献能提升作者的可信度，使作者更好地融入学术共同体。初入科学研究的人经常戏称自己是"科研小白"，白是白纸的白，白意味着对一个领域涉猎不深。征引是和先于我们涉足某个领域的学者建立关联，是对学术对话的确认，确认我们与所征引的人确实发生了某种智慧层面的交流。通过引用权威观点或重要成果，我们得以加入学术共同体，成为"圈内人"。

以上都是征引的合理原因，不过在我看来，征引最重要、最本质的原因还在于论证的需要。我们所征引的文献既可以作为正面的支撑论据，支撑我们的论断②，完成论证；也可以成为反面的论据，我们通过驳倒反面的论据，完成论证。

从论证这一点展开，在广征博引时，我们容易无处安置自己的声音，甚至丢失了自己的声音。这是所有初入学术写作的新手

---

① 颜之推. 颜氏家训［M］. 檀作文，译注. 北京：中华书局，2016：90.
② 我们通常用前提（premises）和结论（conclusions）这组概念来描述文章整体的论证逻辑（详见第二讲）；而在分析某个小的论证单元时，通常用论据（evidence）和论断（claims）这组概念。

几乎都会遇到的困难。下面一个学生的话①，我想也反映了大部分同学的心声。

For me, the big problem is writing an argument. If I give my opinion, then the tutor says "where are your references?" But when I use other authors, then the tutor says "I know what X thinks already— what is your opinion?"

连求学阶段的季羡林也不例外。

隔了大约一个星期，教授在研究所内把文章退还给我，脸上含有笑意，最初并没有说话。我心里咯噔一下，直觉感到情势有点不妙了。我打开稿子一看，没有任何改动，只是在第一行第一个字前面画上了一个前括号，在最后一行最后一个字后面画上了一个后括号。整篇文章就让一个括号括了起来，意思就是说，全不存在了。这真是"坚决、彻底、干净、全部"消灭掉了。这时候教授才慢慢地开了口："你的文章费劲很大，引书不少。但都是别人的意见，根本没有你自己的创见。看上去面面俱到，实际上毫无价值。你重复别人的话，又不完全准确。如果有人对你的文章进行挑剔，从任

---

① GROOM N. "A workable balance": Self and sources in argumentative writing [M]// MITCHELL S, ANDREWS R. Learning to argue in higher education. Portsmouth: Boynton/Cook, 2000: 65-73.

何地方都能对你加以抨击，而且我相信你根本无力还手。因此，我建议，把绪论统统删掉。"①

这个选段来自季羡林先生的《我的第一篇学术论文》，讲的是他在德国留学期间写学位论文的一次经历。在同学们的论文中，有论据无论断，或是有论断无论据的情况并不罕见。请看以下两例。

例1：A study suggested that time is one of the most influential factors that individuals consider when choosing to take the elevator or climb the stairs (Olander & Eves, 2011). Another study revealed that the time of traveling by elevator varies significantly depending on the time of day and day of the week (Shah et al., 2011). In 2013, Bassett et al. (2013) found that if buildings are constructed with centrally located, accessible, and aesthetically pleasing staircases, a greater percentage of people will choose to take the stairs.

例1来自上一讲提到的《哪个更快：爬楼梯还是坐电梯》的论文。引言中的这一段综述了三篇文献。从内容看，和该同学研究的问题十分相关。但作者并没有交代清楚引用这三篇文献的用意是什么，是为了支持一个什么论断。因此，这一段并不是论证，而只是文献的罗列。

---

① 季羡林. 读书・治学・写作 [M]. 杭州：浙江人民出版社，2016: 263-264.

例2：In recent years, with the Internet video platforms developing rapidly, both the population watching online videos and the time consumed by them have skyrocketed. According to Ding et al. (2020), short video users over ten years old in China have reached about 800 million, accounting for more than half of the Chinese population. Meanwhile, acquiring knowledge and broadening horizons through videos have become a trend among young people, especially college students.

例2来自关于"大学生通过网络视频自学效果"这一话题的讨论。在这一小节中，作者交代了讨论的背景，给出了三个论断：(1) 观看网络视频的人数骤增；(2) 人们在观看网络视频上花费的时间骤增；(3) 通过网络获取知识、拓宽眼界已在年轻人，尤其是大学生群体中颇为流行。针对这三个论断，作者仅给了第一个论断一些支持性的数据。因此，这里的论证是非常不充分的。

学术引用关乎自我与他人的平衡。这里的平衡不是跷跷板式的平衡。学术写作中，所引文献的观点是演出时主唱身后的背景音。无论那些声音多么动听，却始终不应取代主唱的位置。主唱自始至终都应该是演出的主角。

如何把自己的声音凸显出来，不让它淹没在文献的汪洋大海中呢？下面，我们来看看《自然》杂志上一篇关于深度学习的文章引言中的一段。

Deep learning is making major advances in solving problems that have resisted the best attempts of the artificial intelligence community for many years. It has turned out to be very good at discovering intricate structures in high-dimensional data and is therefore applicable to many domains of science, business and government. In addition to beating records in image recognition[1-4] and speech recognition[5-7], it has beaten other machine-learning techniques at predicting the activity of potential drug molecules[8], analyzing particle accelerator data[9,10], reconstructing brain circuits[11], and predicting the effects of mutations in non-coding DNA on gene expression and disease[12,13]. Perhaps more surprisingly, deep learning has produced extremely promising results for various task in natural language understanding[14], particularly topic classification, sentiment analysis, question answering[15] and language translation[16,17]. ①

在这个不到 150 词的段落里,作者征引他人文献多达 17 次,但作者并没有被文献牵着鼻子走,而是像战场上的将军一样,始终占据统领地位。作者首先提出自己的论断:深度学习在困扰人工智能领域长达数年的一些问题上正取得突破性的进展。深度学习的优势是能够在高维度的数据中发现精微的结构,在科学、商业和政务领域应用广泛。随后,通过文献征引,我们看到了深度学习在哪些方面打败了其他机器学习技术,以及正大放异彩的具体领域。

不难看出,为凸显自己的声音,作者对文献有归类、整合文献的意识,17 篇文献只占据了约 6 行的篇幅;此外,作者不是把文献孤零零地放在那里,而是与文献深度互动后,在段落开头最显著的位置告诉我们征引这 17 篇文献想要说明的问题,整个段落中也不乏作者自己的声音(如 making major advances, have resisted the best attempts, turn out to be very good at, perhaps more surprisingly)。

如何有效地归类、整合文献?如何与文献深度互动从而呈现自己的声音呢?这里面我想提出学术写作两个很重要的底层能力:笔记和文献批注。

(一)笔记——归类与整合文献

刚开始做研究、写文章,我们并不知道哪些文章有用,哪些

---

① LECUN Y, BENGIO Y, HINTON G. Deep leaning [J]. Nature, 2015, 521: 436-444.

没有。只要看上去有点相关，我们便不假思索地下载下来从头到尾通览一遍。这好比去超市购物时，人们经常走一路买一路，看到新鲜的、打折的都迫不及待地装在购物车上。

在这个阶段，我们可以用"列表式"的方法记笔记。对于理论性文章，尝试提炼作者文章中的一些思想要点。比如，读过 Alastair Pennycook 的"Borrowing others' words: Text, authorship, memory and plagiarism"一文后，我从这篇长达 31 页的文章中，提炼出作者反对的观点放在笔记的上边，作者的观点放在笔记的下边（如图 7-1）；对于实证类文章，按论证的过程组织笔记。比如，读过 Diane Pecorari 的"Good and original: Plagiarism and patchwriting in academic L2 writing"后，我按照研究问题、研究方法、研究结果、研究讨论把笔记分成了四个区域，一一填充相关的信息（如图 7-2）。

图 7-1

图 7-2

使用"列表式"笔记，我的建议是：一篇文章一页 A4 纸。就是文章不论多长，研究多复杂，都要在一页 A4 纸的篇幅将要点呈现出来。

这个"列表式"阶段，我经历了很久。"列表式"笔记能让我们以简约的笔墨留下文章的骨架，即便是几年前读过的文献，也能依靠笔记上的点滴，回忆起研究的大体信息。然而，"列表式"笔记最大的弱点是：当我们写作需要一些观点或数据的细节信息时，还需要再次查阅原文。

当研究和写作的经验渐长，用"列表式"翔实记录过一个小领域几十篇文献后，我们可以尝试采用"标签式"笔记法。"标签式"笔记法的核心，是将文献中有用的信息摘录下来，并赋予该部分信息一个标签。

举个例子。我今年有一个研究生，入学之初发邮件给我说："我发现自己缺乏一定的文献批判能力。在阅读文献时，总是不善于发现其不足之处。"我想这是刚踏入研究领域的学生们普遍面临的困难。我建议她不妨抓住这个问题做一番深入的研究：学生们对待文献的态度和融合文献的实践受到哪些过往读写经历的影响？

在阅读文献的过程中，学生发现卡罗琳·曼特林（Carolyn Matalene）教授在一篇文章提道：在中国的教育传统中，对学生阅读素养的训练很强调复述与背诵，认为复述与背诵是促成知识内化的最有效方式。因此，在我们的教育传统中，是不强调批判性地看待文献的。我们可以给这段话一个标签：教育传统。之后阅读中如再遇到讨论教育传统的，还可以使用这个标签。当积累了一定数量的"教育传统"标签后,我们就可以把具有相同标签的内容都归在一个文档里面。如有必要,再细分类。用标签记录的过程本质上就是写作前对文献细致梳理的过程。

"标签式"笔记法的前提是目的性阅读(purposeful reading)。有目的的阅读和我们之前提到的"通览"不同。目的性阅读能帮助我们大胆舍弃对写作帮助甚微的信息,将阅读迅速定位到可能有引用价值的观点、例证、数据上面。唐君毅先生在《说读书之难与易》中说:"见文字平铺纸上,易;见若干文字自纸面浮起突出,难;见书中文字都是一般大小,易;见书中文字重要性有大有小,而如变大或变小,难。"[1] 这难与易的分水岭就在于目的性阅读。若再以去超市购物类比,用标签法做笔记有如心里似乎装着个购物清单,有目的地游走于各个货架之间,看到想买的东西,仿佛不是我们终于发现了它,而是它映入了眼帘。

然而购物清单易得,笔记的标签从哪里来呢?这个问题可归为如何能实现目的性阅读。

有目的的阅读来自问题意识。问题就像我们心中的一个"结",有了一个"结",我们总想着能解开它。一直盘亘在脑海中的问题,实际上有意无意地帮我们构筑着知识的体系,牵引着思维的方向。

和列表式笔记法相比,标签笔记法是以产出为导向的。当我们有了问题意识,基于目的性阅读采用标签笔记法时,不要寄望一步到位。有时我们对信息重要性的判断可能不合理,在笔记上

---

[1] 唐君毅. 说读书之难与易 [M] //青年与学问. 北京:九州出版社, 2021:20-21.

抄录了一大堆日后看来并不重要的信息，而漏掉了更重要的；有时我们给抄录的文字贴上的那个标签也可能不合理，比如和其他标签的区分度不够，或是同类信息在笔记前后给出了同一标签。但这些都是操练起来更加具体细节的问题，随着我们知识储备的增加和笔记经验的累积都会得以解决。这部分的讲解更多的是方法论上的意义。只要我们确定走在正确的道路上，其他的，尽可以交给时间。

无论列表式还是标签式的笔记，事实上都以我们对记笔记这件事的认同为前提。同学们可能的疑问是，记笔记是不是太浪费时间了。衡量时间是不是被"浪费"了，要看我们站在什么样的视角，以多长的时间跨度去看待了。不少同学不愿意在阅读文献和笔记上下功夫，想引用文献时，就去复制他人文章中引用的文献。这样看上去是"节省"时间了，不过真的是节省了还是浪费了，大家在实践中慢慢地去体会吧。

没有唯一正确的笔记方法。我建议同学们多多尝试不同的笔记方法，在实践中体会哪一种更适合现阶段的自己。无论使用哪一种笔记方法，都要记录好文献的出处。

（二）文献批注——与文献深度互动

我们在上文中说，问题意识是有目的阅读及形成标签的前提。那么问题意识又是从哪里来的呢？为什么读过同样数量的文献，有的同学能够提出很多有趣的问题，而有的同学却提不出任何问题呢？

我认为，这和不同的学术阅读策略相关。学术阅读和我们中小学阶段语文课阅读的侧重点有所不同。学术阅读的重点不在品味和鉴赏，而在与作者对话、向作者质疑，如朱熹言："看人文字，不可随声迁就。我见得是出，方可信。须沉潜玩绎，方有见处。不然，人说沙可做饭，我也说沙可做饭，如何可吃！"[①] 与作者对话、向作者质疑，实际上是在寻求与文献的深度互动。养成文献批注的习惯在这种互动中是非常重要的。

做文献批注的益处是我在很长时间内慢慢体会到的。做批注、留下文字的印记意味着交流真切地发生了。如同冰上的舞者，看上去无比轻盈，但在她所经过的冰面，留下了深深的印记。事实上，在冰刀与冰面接触的地方，有着很强的力，那是真正发生了交互的结果。

如何做文献批注呢？我的建议是从小处着手。一篇学术文章往往有一个大的结论，这个结论是由好多论断（claims）和论据（evidence）构成的，而每个论断下面又有很多小的论断（sub-claims），以及支撑这些小断言的证据（图 7-3）。撼动一棵大树很难，而摘下一面树叶却相对容易。我们训练自己和文献互动的能力时，可以从一些小的论断入手，养成批判性阅读的习惯。

---

① 朱熹. 朱子语类（卷一）[G]. 黎靖德, 编. 王星贤, 点校. 北京：中华书局, 2020：228.

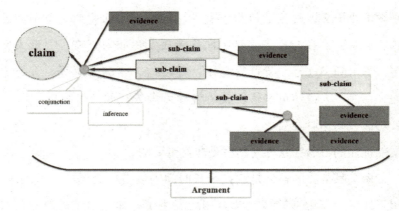

图 7-3 论证的构成

通常来讲，在一个好的论证里，"论据"和"论断"是匹配的。论断的表述以适切为宜。用通俗的话讲，就是"有多大把握就下多大的论断"。我们对自己持有的"论断"深信不疑且证据充分、确凿时，写下的断言也倾向于果断、直接、不留余地；而当我们对自己持有的论断并没有百分之百的把握，比如当论断是基于事实的推测，或是在"一定程度"和"一些情境"下才成立时，往往会使用更为谨慎的断言，增加与人讨论、协商的空间，也就是"话不能说得太死"。

对于论据的评估，可遵循 CRAAP 的标准。CRAAP 是美国图书馆提供的一个批判性辨别信息的方法。五个字母代表了五个标准，依次是：时效性（Current），相关性（Relevant），权威性（Authority），准确性（Accuracy），目的性（Purpose）[①]。

---

① BLAKESLEE S. The CRAAP test [J]. LOEX Quarterly, 2004, 31 (3): 6-7.

下面用一篇发表在《科学美国人》博客专栏中的文章①来说明如何从小处解构一个论证。

这篇标题为"Theorists, experimentalists and the bias in popular physics"的文章指出实验物理学家不如理论物理学家受到的认可度高，并分析了原因。原文第六段开篇如下：

Now there's no doubt that physicists themselves would be the first ones to recognize the value of experimentalists; for instance, Anderson, Davis and the Kendall-Friedman-Taylor trio were all recognized by Nobel Prizes.

第一句话"物理学家会最先认可他们当中实验物理家的贡献，这是毫无疑问的"是该部分的主要论断。我们读到这句话时，不应简单地把它看作一个事实，而应该看作一个论断。面对这个观点，停下来，思考一下：

这个论断果真如作者所言"毫无疑问"（no doubt）吗？
理论物理学家会是最先肯定实验物理学家贡献的人吗？

---

① JOGALEKAR A. Theorist, experimentalist and the bias in popular physics [EB/OL]. (2016-06-03) [2022-11-05]. https://blogs.scientificamerican.com/the-curious-wavefunction/popular-physics-is-there-an-experimentalist-in-the-house/

继续往下阅读，我们看到了作者为支持这一论断所提出的证据：安德森、戴维斯与肯德尔-弗里德曼-泰勒都获得过诺贝尔物理学奖。

面对论据，我们也需要停下来，思考一下：

这个论据是准确的吗？
这个论据和论断足够相关吗？
论据足以支持论断吗？

当我们有这样的疑问时，很可能就会无意识或者有意识地在文章上画些线条，画些问号，零星地写些批注。在这个过程中，我们自身思想的小苗也在潜滋暗长。当批判性阅读成为我们惯常的阅读习惯后，我们"自己的声音"就会越来越清晰可见。

以上，我们谈了学术征引的意义以及如何在浩瀚的文献中与之互动。总结起来，请大家记住下面三句话：

文献使用关乎自我和他人平衡。
文献使用更关乎凸显自己的声音。
文献使用本质上关乎构建一个好的论证。

接下来我们谈谈基于文献写作的另一个重要方面——文献融入（source integration）。当笔记中盛满了潜在有用的信息，接下来就需找到合理的方式融入文献了。文献融入主要有三种方式：直接引用、转述和概述。简单地说，直接引用（direct quotation）是将原文的内容直接引入文章，并用引号明示所引信息；转述（paraphrase）是用自己的话复述原文的内容；概述（summary）是将原文内容加以概括后，融入文章。通常来讲，概述和转述是更高频的融入方式，因为概述和转述呈现了所引文字获得理解与阐释的再语境化过程，更能体现对知识的主动建构。

下面稍加展开，谈一谈使用上述三种方式融入文献时要注意的一些细节。

（1）直接引语

使用直接引语时，要注意引文和原文的"完全一致"。看似题中之义的"完全一致"，却不易落实。我们在直接引用他人文字时，有时不经意间就做了或多或少的改动（如标点、大小写、拼写）。通常来讲，若需要改动原文，哪怕是极细微的方面，也要明示出来。需要掌握省略号和方括号的用法。简单地说，省去了引文中部分文字，要用省略号；改变了引文中文字，则要用方括号。大家可以通过下面的例子看一下直接引用的这些细节。

原文：Nowhere in ESL writing can that pragmatism be better illustrated than in the work that has been done on writing in relation to English for academic purposes. (Santos, 1992: 9)

论文中的引用：Although nearly 30 years have passed since Santos proposed that "[n]owhere in ESL writing can… pragmatism be better illustrated than in the work that has been done on writing in relation to English for academic purposes" (1992: 9), much of current EAP instruction continues to follow a pragmatic approach.

最初在引用这个观点时，我用的是转述，而非直引。后来在修改时，考虑到作者 Terry Santos 是我们领域的知名学者，"Nowhere … can … be better … than …"的表述中带着一些权威感，加之这篇文章年代较久远，把作者的话原汁原味地呈现给读者似乎是更好的选择，我在终稿中把这段引用改为了直接引用。

我们不同意文中观点的时候，也会刻意地选择直接引用，以此和引文保持一定的距离。

(2) 转述

转述包含着一些微技能，比如同义词替代①、词性转换、句式变换，等等。这些都是做好转述的基础。但转述还意味着更多。迪安德罗认为好的转述能够"recast the passage into a freely form version of the original while preserving the essential meaning"②，也就

---

① Word 上面就自带同义词库，要善加利用。也可以使用一些在线的同义词词典。
② D'ANGELO F J. The art of paraphrase [J]. College Composition and Communication, 1979, 30 (3), 255-259.

是在忠实原文核心意义的同时，展现自由的形式。我对这句话的理解是：转述不是对原文简单的拼贴和重组，而要像按自己的语言风格写出的。同学们做转述时，不妨在理解原文后，把想要转述的句子暂且放置一边，等待半分钟或者一分钟后，用自己的话写出来。持续盯着一个句子想方设法地去转述，有时很难摆脱原文语言结构的束缚。

同学们常有的一个困惑是：要转述到什么程度？是不是需要替换掉所有的词？凯克认为好的转述"contain only general words related to the topic and that appear repeatedly in the source text"[①]，即只保留和话题有关的词和原文中总重复出现的词。可见，转述并非要对所有词都加以转化。我们可以保留和话题有关的词和总重复出现的词。总重复出现的词往往是专业术语。保持全文术语表述统一是重要的。

（3）概述

最后说说概述。概述是对原文信息梗概的表述，因此概述的过程本质上是信息压缩的过程。概述对同学们应该一点都不陌生。从小学到高中语文课上"归纳中心思想"的练习，就是对概述技能的训练。概述也渗透在我们生活的方方面面。和久别的好友重逢，往往第一句话是："近来如何？"因故缺席了一堂课，会问刚听课回来的室友："今天老师都讲了些啥？"这些问题于听话者，

[①] KECK C. The use of paraphrase in summary writing: A comparison of L1 and L2 writers [J]. Journal of Second Language Writing, 2006, 15(4): 261-278.

都需要把较长时间线上的信息整合压缩，加以提炼。

概述考验的功夫，第一是取舍。我们平时在学术论文中看到的摘要（abstract），本质上是对整篇论文的一个概述。我们把几千字的论文提炼成一两百字的摘要，绝大部分的内容都舍掉了。我建议同学们通读一篇论文，读完自己写一份摘要，再和原摘要去比较，然后观察在信息的取舍上自己和原文作者有哪些异同。经过几次这样的练习，你会对摘要写作更有信心。

概述还需要些凝练提升的功夫。语言系统中有一个大大的语义网，我们可以思考需要概述的段落中一些重要信息的类属，看看能否用一些不在句子当中的较为抽象的上位词来提炼句子的内核。苹果、梨、香蕉的上位词是水果，微信、QQ 的上位词是社交软件，按照这样的思路，上升、下降说的都是趋势（trend）；防水、防潮说的都是特性（features）；还有背景、功能、规律、优势、不足、方向等具有概括性意义的词，都可以装进我们概述的词汇库里。

无论采用上述哪种方式融入文献，我们要遵循两点共同的原则：

1. 要准确。
2. 要相关。

准确就是"信"，尤其在转述和概述的时候，要如实地反映原文的意思，不可断章取义，更不可无中生有。做到这点很是不易，很多时候,"曲解"他人的意思并非有意为之,而是我们的知识积累还不够,不能根据作者所处的时代背景和学术背景,准确理解作者的意思。

相关就是"切",这里我给大家推荐 Research Gate 这个网站。这个网站有一个很好的功能,就是可以看到一篇文章在其他作者那里的引用情况。通过观察,我们可以很清晰地看到:即便是对同一句话的转述,同一篇引文的概述,不同文章会呈现出非常不同的面貌。以概述为例,引用中突出某篇文章的理论创新、方法创新还是结果,这完全取决于论文作者自身行文的需要。这也是为什么我们在引用他人文章内容时,要尽可能读原文。二手文献里别人已经做好的直接引用、转述或概述,不一定符合我们文章的需要。

最后我们简要谈谈学术写作的征引规范。

现代学术的征引规范是在科学研究的发展过程中渐渐形成的。学术征引大体分为两种类型:一是人名—日期式(author-date style),二是数字角标式(numeric style)。人名—日期式能凸显理论、观点的提出者以及时间上的承继关系,为人文社科领域青睐;数字角标式淡化被征引者,更凸显研究成果本身,在自然科学领域广泛使用。这两种类型在文内引用和文后引用中还分为不同的格式(如 APA,MLA,Chicago),很多期刊也有其专属格式。

看似简单的文献征引,里面却有不少细致之处:作者有两人、三人、三人以上时如何征引?二手文献如何征引?一个作者同年发表了两篇文章如何征引?两个作者姓氏相同如何征引?这些不打算向大家一一介绍了,手头常备所在学科最新版的学术写作格式规范手册(比如心理学领域的 APA 手册①),遇到问题随时查阅,我认为是最有效的方法。

---

① American Psychological Association. Publication manual of the American Psychological Association［M］. Washington, D. C.: American Psychological Association, 7th edition, 2020.

本讲练习

1. 下面表格中所列的七种情形①属于剽窃吗？请用"√"表明最符合你的观点的选项。

> 1=definitely not plagiarized; 2=more than likely not plagiarized; 3=likely not plagiarized; 4=unsure; 5=likely to be plagiarized; 6=more than likely to be plagiarized; 7=definitely plagiarized

	1	2	3	4	5	6	7
Quoting someone's language without acknowledgment							
Quoting someone's ideas without acknowledgement							
Quoting Internet sources without acknowledgement							
Copying a paragraph verbatim from someone's writing without acknowledgement							
Incorporating someone's ideas into one's own writing without acknowledgement							
Expressing someone's ideas in one's own language without acknowledgement							
Synthesizing information from a number of sources without acknowledgement							

---

① HU G W, LEI J. Investigating Chinese University Students' Knowledge of and Attitudes toward Plagiarism from an Integrated Perspective [J]. Language Learning, 2012, 62 (3): 813-850.

2. 请你在 Research Gate 网站上面搜索一篇被引用 10 次以上的文献，观察其他文献是如何概述这篇文献的，这些概述有何异同？试着分析其中的原因。

3. 请阅读本专业的一篇研究综述，分析作者如何通过有效的引用，凸显自己的声音。

第八讲　数　据

这一讲，我们谈一谈基于数据的写作。

数据这个词的英文是 data，是 datum 的复数形式。在学术文章中经常出现的就是这个复数的形式。

什么是数据呢？数据是可作为推理、讨论、计算基础的事实性信息。这里有两个关键点，数据一定是"事实性信息"，因此在实验设计的阶段，我们要考虑如何能让所得数据，最大程度地反映现实。切不可伪造、捏造数据。另外一个关键词是"基础"，数据就像我们建房子的原材料，有了它，日后的一些推理、讨论和计算才有源头。

基于数据的写作我们主要讲两个方面，一个是数据可视化（Data Visualization），另一个是数据评述（Data Commentary）。

先来看数据可视化。数据可视化，简单地说，就是用图形呈现数据，从而帮助读者更好地理解数据。学术论文中，数据可视化最常用的是表（tables）和图（figures）[1]。表是网格状，有一定数量的行与列。表之外的图形都可归为图。图大体分两类，一类

---

[1] 英文通常用 graphics 一词来统称表和图。

是 chart，一类是 graph，中文都叫"图"，但它们略有区别。Chart 通常有比较明确的形状，比如柱状图（bar chart）、饼状图（pie chart）、流程图（flow chart）等；而 graph 通常由连续不间断的线构成，最常见的就是折线图（line graph）了。

不同类型的图表各有所长。什么时候该用哪一种呢？我们来看一个例子。下方的一个表和两张图描述的是同样的信息：2011—2020 年这 10 年间北京市居民出生、死亡变动情况①。

表 8-1 2011—2020 年北京市居民出生、死亡变动情况

年份	2011	2012	2013	2014	2015	2016	2017	2018	2019	2020
出生数（人）	110033	132227	127015	152929	126648	147789	171305	140921	132634	100368
死亡数（人）	75125	77445	80113	82641	86007	89599	93154	96418	97112	97649

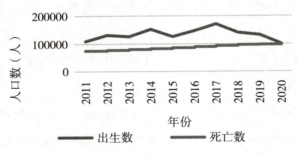

图 8-1 2011—2020 年北京市居民出生、死亡变动情况

---

① 北京市卫生健康大数据与政策研究中心. 1949—2021 年北京市居民出生、死亡变动情况［EB/OL］.（2021-03-28）［2022-11-07］http://www.phic.org.cn/tjsj/wssjzy/jkzb/202203/t20220328_299557.html

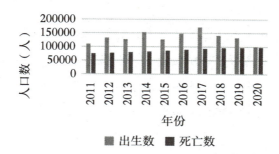

图 8-2　2011—2020 年北京市居民出生、死亡变动情况

不难看出，表和图各有优势。表格精确，读者可以很容易从表中获取一些具体的、离散的数值信息。线形图可呈现随时间变化的趋势，而柱状图则更容易让我们看到在同一个时间段，不同组别之间的区别。因此，为数据选择合理的呈现方式，是数据可视化的题中之义。

图表往往是最能吸引读者注意的部分，要确保它的规范、美观。无论选取哪种图表形式，都需要注意下面几点：

> 图/表要在同一页显示，一张图/表通常不分居两页。
> 三线表（顶线、底线、栏目线）因形式简明、可读性强在学术论文中被广泛采用。需要掌握三线表的制作方法。
> 图表的标题通常有比较固定的位置，要符合所在学科和期刊的惯例。
> 图表中每个数据都要有单位（如表 8-1 中出生人口若用 11.0, 13.2 等记，则单位要用"万人"表示）。

➢ 要明示图例和坐标轴的含义。
➢ 用不同颜色区分不同数据时，要确保黑白打印时依然有足够的区分度。
➢ 不同画图软件的默认字体和字号有所不同，要尽量确保不同图表都和正文中文字的字体和大小保持一致。

接下来，我们来看基于数据写作的另一个重要方面：数据评述。数据评述不同于数据描述。数据描述只需要如实介绍图表中呈现出来的数据。可问题是，既然图表已直观而清晰地呈现了数据，再用文字重复一遍的意义是什么呢？我认为，基于数据的写作和第七讲基于文献的写作殊途同归：论证的需要。具体地说，呈现数据不是终极目的，我们需要把数据当作证据，支持自己的论点。

下面我们通过一个例子来看看好的数据评述长什么样子。下例来自塞尔温教授发表于《社会科学计算机评论》的一个研究[1]。1222名美国大学生汇报了自己在过去的12个月里上网时有哪些不当或违法行为，以及这些行为的频次。

---

[1] SELWYN N. A safe haven for misbehaving? An investigation of online misbehavior among university students [J]. Social Science Computer Review, 2008, 26, 446-465.

Table 2　University Student Respondents' Self-Reported Instances of Online Misbehavior during the Previous 12 Months (N=1222)

		Once or Twice	A Few Times	More Than a Few Times	Overall Percentage
Misrepresentation of self	Given false information about yourself to another person on the internet	34.0	12.0	5.0	51.0
	Provided false information about your personal details on an online form	33.0	13.0	5.0	51.0
Unauthorized use of another's account	Accessed someone else's email account without his or her knowledge	18.0	6.0	2.0	26.0
	Used someone's credit details online without his or her knowledge	4.0	1.0	1.0	6.0
Plagiarism of an essay or assignment	Copied a few sentences from a website into an essay or assignment without citing the source	39.0	16.0	5.0	60.0
	Copied a few paragraphs from a website into an essay or assignment without citing the source	21.0	7.0	2.0	30.0
	Copied a few pages from a website into an essay or assignment without citing the source	8.0	3.0	1.0	12.0
	Copied a whole essay or assignment from a website without citing the source	2.0	1.0	0.6	4.0
	Paid for an essay or assignment from a website	2.0	0.7	0.7	3.0
Unauthorized downloading of music or film	Unauthorized downloading of music from the internet	18.0	22.0	36.0	76.0
	Unauthorized downloading of film or video from the internet	18.0	16.0	19.0	53.0
Pornography use	Viewed online pornography or pornographic pictures or films	17.0	12.0	11.0	40.0
	Paid for online pornography or pornographic pictures or films	3.0	1.0	1.0	5.0

这张表上呈现了很多数据，细数足有 52 个。那么，我们该如何评述这张表呢？需要把所有数据都呈现给读者吗？

下面一段文字是关于上表的数据评述。共 10 句话。我们逐句分析一下。

(1) Table 2 shows survey respondents' self-reported involvement in online misbehavior during the previous 12 months. (2) According to the table, the most common online misbehavior is "unauthorized downloading of film and music." (3) As can be seen, just over three out of four students in the study have downloaded music or film more than once a year. (4) This very high percentage of misbehavior is especially alarming, since protection of intellectual property is a basic element for enriching the film and music industries. (5) Another notable result is that viewing pornographic materials on the internet was reported by 40% of the respondents, although purchasing pornography was reported by only a small minority of these respondents. (6) The least frequently reported misbehaviors were illegally using another person's email account or credit information, along with either completely copying homework from a website or buying an assignment from a source on the internet. (7) It is worthwhile to note that these different forms of online misbehavior seems to be patterned

> according to the degree of the perceived seriousness of the bad behavior. (8) Activities that are generally believed to be criminal (e. g., using someone's credit information) were less frequent than activities that, although unlawful, many do not view as criminal, such as downloading movies and music. (9) Illegal downloading may have an economic cause, but other reasons might be important, as well. (10) This problem will likely to continue until reasons that students engage in this behavior are clearly identified.

首句中,作者介绍了图表的位置(Table 2 shows)和主要内容信息。由于排版的原因,很多图表不一定和文字紧密相连,因此在文字中交代图表准确的位置信息非常重要。为清晰起见,尽量不要用"由下面这张表可知""参见上面的图"这样的表述。

图表的位置信息可装在主动句里(如此例),还可装在被动句里(如例1)、括号里(如例2)。

例1:The types of internet misbehavior common among university students are shown in Table 2.

例2:The types of internet misbehavior common among university students are shown (see Table 2).

此外，作者介绍图表内容时，对图表的题目做了一定的转写。

第二句汇报了该研究最主要的结果之一，并在第三句中用数据支持了这一结果。第五、六句汇报了另外两个主要的结果。可见，作者并没有在数据评述中汇报所有的结果，而是有所取舍。

此句还请大家注意作者汇报数据时的语言特点。第三句的 just over three out of four，第五句的 40% 和 only a small minority 中，40% 这个数据和原文完全一致，其他两处则做了变化。Just over three out of four 对应表格里的数据是 76%；Only a small minority 对应表格里的数据是 5%。作者为什么做这样的变化呢？

举个例子：如果我们说一种疾病的发病率约 76%，读者可能没有太多的感受；但用了 three out of four，给人的感觉是四个人中就会有三个人害病，这种病的高发病率变得真切可感了。可见，数据是不会自己说话的，我们介绍数据时的表达方式，不知不觉赋予了数据意义。文中的 5% 是个很客观的数据，作者想强调 5% 是个很低的比例时，会说 only a small minority。大家想一想，如果想强调 5% 并不低会怎样表达呢？

再来看第七、八句。我认为这两句是整个段落当中写得最精彩的两句，很能体现数据评述的特点。数据是散乱的，我们作为作者需要从散乱的数据中发现规律和趋势。第七句就是对数据当中趋势、规律性的揭示，关键词就是 pattern；第八句则是对规律、趋势形成原因的推测。

我们需要注意第七句中 seem to be 这个表达[①]。第七句是作者

---

① 和 seem to be 这个表达功能类似的，还有 tend to, appear to 等。

基于数据的断言。作者在下断言时,采取了一种比较审慎的态度。使用 seem to be,看上去削弱了断言的力量,实则为断言留下了余地,为可能相异的观点留下了对话的空间。当我们的断言更加合理、更经得起推敲时,整个论证也就更容易让人信服了。

最后来看第九、十句。这两句所述的内容既不是对结果的呈现,也不是某种规律性的总结,而是作者在得到结果后,对背后原因的分析,对未来趋势的判断和研究方向的预测。这些也是数据评述的重要组成部分。如同书评、影评,数据评述中数据本身固然重要,但读者往往更想看到的是作者对数据的解读、评价、预测、展望等。这就要求作者能把数据放在整个研究领域去探讨。比如第十句的后半部分 until reasons that students engage in this behavior are clearly identified,这句话看上去是个简单的陈述,但稍加分析,可得出这句话潜在含义是:目前对学生此般行为的原因并不十分明了。事实上,这句话为未来的研究指明了一个方向。

此外,第九、十句中的 may 和 likely 也值得关注。这两句中的 may 和 likely 是对可能性的提示。作者虽然对结果产生的原因做了分析,对未来发展趋势做了预测,但通过 may 和 likely 提示读者:这只是我的一家之言,欢迎不同观点加入讨论。

通过这个例子,我们看到了数据评述需要包括的主要内容:(1)给读者指明图表位置,介绍图表主要内容;(2)用数据作为支撑,汇报主要的发现,对数据体现的趋势、规律等做出归纳;(3)数据评述:包括对某个数据出现原因的分析,基于数据的展望,指明未来的研究方向等。

讲完了这个范例，我给大家看看三个同学就 2011—2020 年北京市居民出生、死亡变动情况所写的数据评述。

A 同学的数据评述

Table 8-1 lists the survey results of the newborn and death population of residents in Beijing from 2011 to 2020. We found that the newborn and death population of Beijing residents from 2011 to 2020 showed different patterns of change. It can be seen that the number of annual newborns from 2011 to 2017 displayed a wave-like increase. In 2014, the growth rate was the greatest compared with the previous year, which was 20.4%. The newborn population of residents reached the highest value of more than 170,000 in 2017, but the newborn population in the three years after 2017 decreased year by year. The newborn population in 2018 and 2020 decreased by more than 30,000 compared with the previous year. The newborn population in 2020 is even less than the newborn population in 2011.

On the contrary, the death population showed an overall increasing tendency, but the annual increase rate varied, with the year 2018 being an obvious inflection point. The death population between 2011 and 2018 increased by about 3,000 per year,

> while the death population increased by only around 600 from 2018 to 2020, indicating that there may be a tendency for fewer deaths in the coming years.

A 同学的数据评述在对图表信息的识别和呈现上做得很不错。文中基于具体的数据，给出了下面一些论述（statement），包括：

… the newborn and death population of Beijing residents from 2011 to 2020 showed different patterns of change.

… the number of annual newborns from 2011 to 2017 displayed a wave-like increase.

… the death population showed an increasing tendency, but the annual increase rate varied, with the year 2018 being an obvious inflection point.

但比较遗憾的是，作者基于这些论断给出的数据评述仅有最后一句话中的 indicating that there may be a tendency for fewer deaths in the coming years，显得比较单薄。

B 同学的数据评述

Figure 8-1 shows new births and deaths of the resident population in Beijing from 2011 to 2020. The new births of the resident population in the upper part of the figure present an interesting data change. During this decade, the newborn populations change like two peaks sandwiching a valley. There are apparent peaks in 2014 and 2017, while in the middle of these two years, the number of new-borns in 2015 does not steadily increase but suddenly decreases.

This phenomenon may be related to national policies and folk customs. Firstly, China implemented the policy of "two-child fertility policy for couples where either the husband or the wife is from a single-child family" in November 2013 and the "the universal two-child policy" in January 2016, respectively, which promoted the increase in the birth population in the following year. Secondly, zodiac preference may affect some families' pregnancy plans. 2015 is the Lunar Year of the Sheep, and some families have cases of early or delayed childbearing. For example, in July 2015, the number of registered pregnant women in Beijing increased significantly, with a year-on-year increase of 21%.

Another notable trend is that the number of births has declined since 2017, reaching the lowest value in 2020, even less than two-thirds of the peak. Many long-term factors influence this development trend. Affected by comprehensive factors such as changes in the economic and social environment, rising direct and indirect costs of bringing up children, and changes in labor and employment patterns, Chinese residents' concept of marriage and childbearing and related behaviors are in recent years changing. The number of late in marriage, late in childbearing, celibatarian, and DINK is gradually increasing, and the size of the childbearing age population is decreasing, resulting in a decrease in the birth rate of our country in recent years. In addition, the COVID-19 sudden outbreak since the end of 2019 has also brought some uncertainty to the population development trend. The low newborn population growth exposes the pressure of population development and further highlights the structural problems of the population. How to promote the long-term balanced development of the population has become a challenging problem for the government.

In contrast to the fluctuating pattern of the newborn population, the death population is slowly rising in general. One of the reasons may be that the first generation of baby boomers, those born in 1949-1958, entered old age in 2009-2018. In the following three years, from 1959 to 1961, the national food shortage crisis caused by three years of natural disasters resulted in a lower birth rate than the baby boom period, which may have a certain impact on the death rate after 2018. With the second generation of baby boomers about to enter old age and China's huge population base, the death population in the future may continue to increase.

B同学这篇数据评述的最大优点是内容充实，结构清晰：第一、二、三自然段评述了出生人口的变化情况；第四自然段评述了死亡人口的变化情况。首先，在对出生人口变化的评述中，该同学用 two peaks sandwiching a valley 非常形象地描述了这十年人口变化的主要特点。之后对这个特点的解释中，先是从国家宏观的生育政策角度分析了两个波峰的出现，而后从生肖避讳的角度分析了波谷的出现。生肖避讳是不是这个波谷出现的原因？这里，作者给出了一个证据：在 2015 年 7 月，北京的登记孕妇人数明显增加，同比增长 21%。与此同时，生肖避讳对这个波谷出现的解释力有多强？作者用 may affect 为自己的论断留下了余地，也打开了对话和进一步探讨的空间。

之后作者用了整整一段分析了在人口政策愈加宽松的大背景下，出生人口数却出现了断崖式下降的原因。作者列举了众多原因，包括经济和社会环境变化、抚养子女直接和间接成本增加、劳动就业方式变化、婚育观念变化、育龄人口规模不断缩小、疫情的影响等。在这一段的末尾，作者指出了低生育率带来的人口结构性问题和挑战。

在最后一段对死亡人口变化情况的数据评述里，作者展现了很好的历史观，提到了1949年后的"婴儿潮"对2010—2020年死亡人口的影响。值得一提的是，作者看到了死亡人口的增加在2018年之后似乎有放缓的趋势，并结合三年严重困难的历史事实分析了这一现象。最后，作者对未来死亡人数的变化作出了预期。

C 同学的数据评述

> Fig. 8-1 shows the population of residents in Beijing from 2011 to 2020. The newborn population in Beijing from 2010 to 2017 experienced a fluctuating increase, with the number of new births reaching its peak in 2017. After 2017, the number of new births began to decline yearly. In 2020, The population of new births is only 58 percent of that in 2017. Unlike the fluctuations in the number of new births, the annual number of deaths from 2011 to 2020 increases year by year at a small rate. The numbers of new births and new deaths are almost the same in 2020.

The main driving force of population growth before 2017 came from economic growth and the "two-child" policy implemented[1-2]. As regards the unusual drop in the number of new births in 2015, experts from the National Health Commission believe it is mainly due to zodiac preferences (being born in the Year of "Sheep" will bring people bad luck)[3]. According to one survey reported by the Commission, Beijing's number of pregnant women filing in the second half of 2015 increased by more than 40% compared to the same period the previous year.

As for the drop in the number of new births after 2017, the establishment of Xiong'an New Area[4] may result in the outflow of young people. However, the nationwide decrease of new births after 2017[5] suggests the outflow is not likely to be the top reason. The high cost of living and childbearing, and the reluctance of getting married may account better for this drop.

Moreover, the number of deaths is increasing year by year because the population base is increasing. The slow growth rate can be attributed to the increasing life expectancy.

Looking into the future, Beijing's new-birth number may experience a further cliff-like decline due to the economic downturn brought by the COVID-19 pandemic. It can be predicted that Beijing's population will likely show negative growth for the first time in 2021.

References:

[1] The State Council Information Office of the People's Republic of China. (2013). *The Decision of the Central Committee of the Communist Party of China on Several Major Issues of Comprehensively Deepening Reform.* The State Council Information Office of the People's Republic of China. http://www.scio.gov.cn/zxbd/nd/2013/Document/1374228/1374228_10.htm

[2] The State Council Information Office of the People's Republic of China (2015). *Communiqué of the Fifth Plenary Session of the 18th Central Committee of the Communist Party of China.* The State Council Information Office of the People's Republic of China. http://www.scio.gov.cn/ztk/dtzt/2015/33995/33999/34093/Document/1466038/1466038.htm

[3] National Health Commission of the People's Republic of China. (2016). *Head of Guidance Department answers questions from Health News and China Population News on the number of births in 2015.* Central People's Government of the People's Republic of China. http://www.nhc.gov.cn/jczds/s3582r/201601/c44109e11fdc4a3dbca337742da86fc3.shtml

[4] Xinhua News Agency (2017). *The Central Committee of the Communist Party of China and the State Council decided to establish the Xiong'an New Area in Hebei.* Xinhua News Agency, http://www.xinhuanet.com/2017-04/01/c_1120741584.htm

> [5] National Bureau of Statistics (n.d.). *Population birth rate, death rate, and natural growth rate.* National Bureau of Statistics. https://data.stats.gov.cn/easyquery.htm? cn=C01

　　C 同学的这篇数据评述和 B 同学采用了不同的结构,但同样十分清晰:作者在第一自然段将出生和死亡人口在过去十年的变化趋势做了整体的描述,紧接着在第二、三、四自然段对变化趋势的特点做了具体分析,最后作者对未来人口变化的趋势做出了预测。

　　如果大家把 B 同学和 C 同学对出生人口变化原因的分析放在一起比较,不难发现,C 同学分析出的原因和 B 同学有很多相似之处,但 C 同学明示了一些政策、观点、结果的出处,体现了论证的过程。

　　特别值得称赞的是,这位同学使用的论据多是来自官方网站的一手资料。关于"二孩"政策,作者给出的文献的出处是由国务院新闻办公室发布、2013 年 11 月 12 日中国共产党第十八届中央委员会第三次全体会议通过的《中共中央关于全面深化改革若干重大问题的决定》和 2015 年 10 月 29 日中国共产党第十八届中央委员会第五次全体会议通过的《中国共产党第十八届中央委员会第五次全体会议公报》;关于生肖避讳的观点,给出的是国家卫生计生委计划生育基层指导司负责人就 2015 年出生人口数答《健康报》《中国人口报》记者时给出的观点;关于雄安新区的设立,给出的是新华社于 2017 年 4 月 1 日受权发布的《中共中央、国务院决定设立河北雄安新区》；关于 2017 年之后全国出生人口的变化，给出的是国家统计局网站的数据。通过引用权威文献，论证的可信度大大地增强了。

事实上，实证性学术论文的结果部分就是由若干数据评述构成的。抛开学术论文，在这个大数据时代，能从数据中获取有效信息和解读分析信息也是我们需要具备的能力。

本讲练习

1. 从本专业的书籍或期刊中找到至少三个带图表的文字段落，并回答：

（1）这是一个什么图表？（如：柱状图；流程图；直方图）

（2）这个图表的出处是哪里？（如：官方数据；实验数据）

（3）文字段落中是如何提及这张图表的？

2. 仔细阅读下面的一张图，写一段 200—250 字的数据评述。数据评述需要包含下面几方面的信息：（1）简要介绍背景话题及图片信息；（2）描述重要的数据、特征、趋势等；（3）推测数据、特征、趋势背后的原因和可能产生的影响（如果使用了外部文献，需要给出文献出处）。

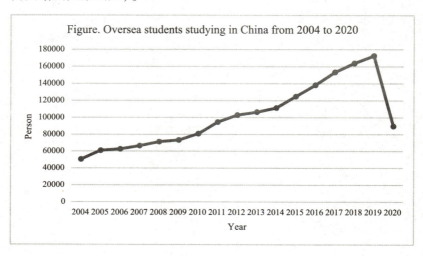

Source: National Bureau of Statistics of China

第九讲　工　具

小说家斯蒂芬·金在《写作这回事》① 里讲了一个关于工具箱的故事。一次，他家窗户的隔扇坏了，需要修理。他的姨父②奥伦把一个三层工具箱从车库拖过整幢房子，从装满各种锤子、锯子、钳子、扳手、电钻等工具的第一层拿出了一把螺丝刀。金很不解，为什么不把螺丝刀直接放在裤子后面的口袋呢？

他的姨父答他："但是我到了这边万一发现还需要别的东西呢，对不对？最好把工具带在身边。不然你如果碰到意料之外的问题，就很容易会因为没准备而气馁。"

由此，金先生给我们的建议是："你为了尽最大的能力写作，有必要建造自己的工具箱，然后增强肌肉力量，才有力气把箱子带在身边。你这样做，就不必在面对艰难任务时感到气馁，而是一把抓过适用的工具，立刻投入工作。"

这一讲，我们讲讲学术写作中的工具。

---

① 斯蒂芬·金. 写作这回事：创作生涯回忆录 [M]. 张坤，译. 北京：人民文学出版社，2016: 95.
② 金当时住在姨妈艾瑟琳和姨父奥伦位于缅因州德翰姆的家里。

（一）拼写、标点、语法检查

下面这个段落是一篇关于微生物疗法论文的摘要。你能发现里面的拼写、标点、语法错误吗？

Abstract

Microbiological therapy is a promising therapy employing bactera to treat diseases, but its development is hindered by several kinds of factors. Although the achievements and good prospects of this therapy are proposed, few studies have sought to specifically analyze the factors hindering its development. To systematically explore those factors, we do questionnaire surveys for the public. Analysis of the data is based on the specially designed model to obtain scientific results. The results show that the public are concerned about microbiological therapy due to their little knowledge of it and the risk of this new technology, which suggests researchers to pay more attention on public awareness when applying a new technology. The findings of this study are of a great significance to contribute to develop microbiological therapy.

我们在电脑上打字，拼错单词是常有的事。Word 里自带拼写检查功能，要善加利用。Word 也提供语法检查，但能检出的问题比较有限。建议大家下载一款专业的语法纠错软件 Grammarly（www.grammarly.com）。

从下图可见，Grammarly 共检查出了 1 处拼写错误和 7 处语法错误，并用红线标记了出来。

Abstract

Microbiological therapy is a promising therapy employing bactera to treat diseases, but its development is hindered by several kinds of factors. Although achievements and good prospects of this therapy are proposed, few studies have specifically analyze the factors hindering its development. To systematically explore these factors, we do questionnaire surveys for the public. Analysis of the data is based on the specially designed model to obtain scientific results. The results show that the public are concerned about microbiological therapy due to their little knowledge of it and the risk of this new technology, which suggests researchers to pay more attention on public awareness when applying a new technology. The findings of this study are of a great significance to contribute to develop microbiological therapy.

图 9-1　Grammarly 为一段摘要提供的语法检查

针对每一处错误，Grammarly 也给出了修改建议，具体如下：

错误	修改建议
bactera	bacteria
the specifically	a specifically
are	is
to	to
on	to
a new	a new
a great significance	a great significance
develop	developing

Grammarly 不仅能帮助我们修改,还能提供对于修改建议的解释。这对于我们积累词汇和语法知识十分有益。希望大家在提交课程论文及给期刊投稿前,主动扫清基本的语言错误。

(二)词语的选择

我常常问同学们:怎样才算学会一个单词?这个问题可以换一种说法:"一个单词里有什么?"

在我看来,一个单词里有:

> ➢ 形式(form)。
> ➢ 意义(meaning)。
> ➢ 词性(part of speech/word class)。
> ➢ 词簇(word family)。
> ➢ 同义词/反义词(synonym/antonym)。
> ➢ 搭配(collocation),即一个单词和什么样的词经常搭配在一起使用。
> ➢ 联想意义(connotation),即一个单词是具有褒义的(positive connotation)、贬义的(negative connotation),还是中性的(neutral)意义。
> ➢ 语体风格(style),即一个单词使用的情境和场合。比如这个单词通常用在书面的、正式的场合,还是用在口语的、非正式的场合。

关于一个单词的形式(拼写、发音)、意义、词性和词簇的知识，很容易从词典上获得，但同义词/反义词，以及关乎单词使用(搭配、联想意义，语体等)的知识通常不容易从普通词典上获得。下面向大家介绍一下同义词词典以及几个与单词用法相关的工具。

1. 同义词词典(thesaurus)

当我们需要转述或概述别人的话语时，通常会在词的层面，寻找同义词替换。很多同学不知道 word 在"审阅"菜单下的同义词库。比如我们输入替换(substitute)这个词，就出现了二十余个它的同义词。

除了 word 自带的同义词库，我们还可以利用同义词网站(如 www.freethesaurus.com)。下图是 free thesaurus 这个网站提供的 altruistic 一词的同义词(也包括几个用方块标示的反义词)。

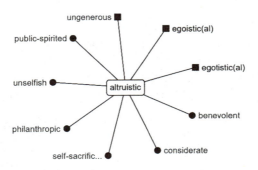

图 9-2 free thesaurus 网站提供的 altruistic 一词的同义词/反义词

还有一些网站(如 https://www.thesaurus.com)提供同义词比较

的功能，有助于我们在众多同义词中做出选择。

补充一句，学术写作中一些关键的概念、术语不需要替换同义词，这也是学术写作力求准确、清晰的需要。

2. Linggle

作为汉语母语者，我们在长期的语言浸泡和熏染中，拥有了对母语的敏感。比方我们知道"提高效率"是好的搭配，而"加强效率"不是好的搭配；我们知道"顽强"与"顽固"、"成果"与"后果"在情感色彩上的细微差别；我们还知道"走了""逝世""死亡"用在不同的场合。

英语不是我们的母语，我们恐怕在上述几个方面没有母语者那样的敏感度。写作时，我们不妨寻求一些写作工具的帮助，比如 Linggle (https://www.linggle.com/) ①可以帮助我们很好地解决搭配方面的问题。现举两例说明。

例：The table shows all the information relevant to costs.

我在第六讲"用词"提到用词的原则之一是简洁，那么如何把 relevant to 换为形式上更简单的介词呢？你可能想到了 about, of, 或是 on。那么，到底哪个和 information 搭配在英语里更常见？我们把三种搭配都输入搜索栏，用斜线区隔开。从图 9-3 中，不难发现，information 后面接续 about 和 on 这两个介词的频率明显比

---

① Linggle 由台湾清华大学自然语言处理实验室于 2008 年开发。

of 更高。

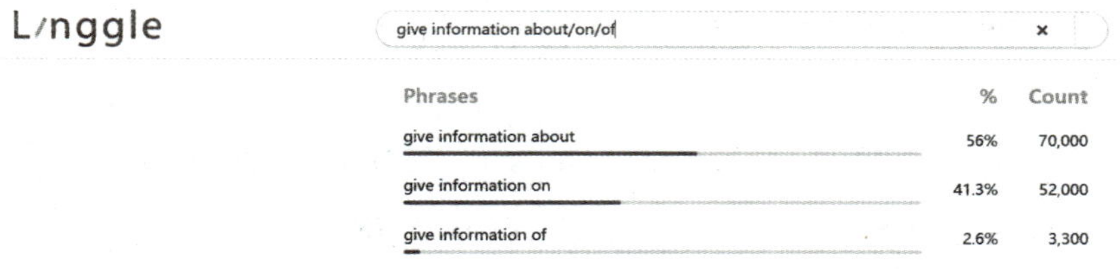

图 9-3　Linggle 网站上"give information"后面常用的介词频率对比

再如，在中文中我们用量词"束""道""线"来界定光线，如"一束光"，或"一道光""一线光"，那么英文中对应的词是什么呢？这个问题使用 Linggle 也不难解决（见图 9-4）。

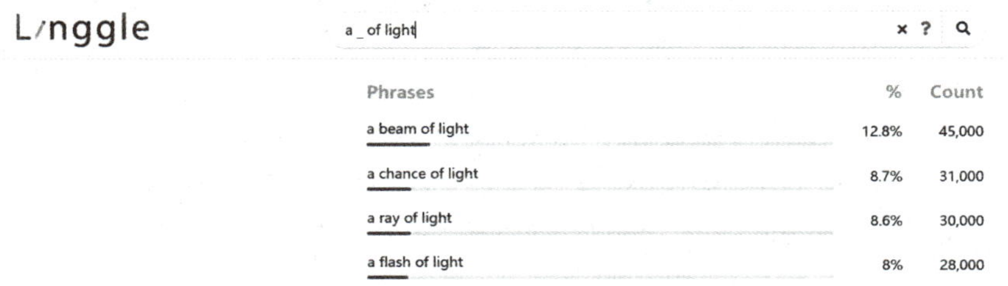

图 9-4　Linggle 网站上"一束光"的英文表达

3. SKELL

当我们需要基于完整的句子更好地了解一个单词的用法时，SKELL（https://www.sketchengine.eu/skell/）是个好帮手。

一次，我在课上讲了 elicit 这个单词，请同学们写一个句子。当走到离我最近的一个同学那时，我看到他写下的句子是这样的：

Since I like to sit in front of the class, teachers always elicit me to answer questions.

英文中是否有"elicit sb. to do sth"这样的用法呢？我们来看看 SKELL 语料库上提供的关于 elicit 的一些例句。

elicit 4.53 hits per million

1. The flashing smile it **elicited** was wholly feral.
2. But familiar calls often **elicited** an immediate response.
3. Neither seemed able to **elicit** any information.
4. Physical collateral can still **elicit** an emotional response.
5. Simple main effects were evaluated if a significant interaction was **elicited**.
6. Even acknowledging already manifest public fear can **elicit** this criticism.
7. Each chemical **elicited** different frequency and amplitude patterns and different behaviors.
8. Sound can be **elicited** via electrical stimulation.
9. Several post training benefits of the training were **elicited**.
10. These perceptions **elicit** various emotions that are specific to each person.
11. Adventure therapy encompasses varying techniques and environments to **elicit** change.
12. The text books deliberately **elicit** the same responses to every lesson.

图 9-5 SKELL 上列举的包含 elicit 一词的句子

从图 9-5 可见，elicit 的对象可以是 smile, response, information, interaction, criticism, frequency, patterns, behaviors, stimulation, benefits, emotion, change，可见这个单词通常是不与人称代词的宾格（me, him, her, them）连用的。

图 9-6 为我们展示了在 SKELL 的语料库中，和动词 elicit 搭配强度最靠前的一些名词。这和我们刚才通过例句的归纳是高度吻合的。

	object of elicit	
1.	response	elicit a response
2.	sympathy	elicit sympathy
3.	reaction	elicit a reaction
4.	laughter	elicit laughter
5.	emotion	emotions elicited
6.	confession	to elicit confessions
7.	laugh	elicit laughs
8.	reply	elicited a reply
9.	behavior	elicit behaviors
10.	feedback	elicit feedback
11.	criticism	elicited criticism
12.	fear	elicit fear

图 9-6　SKELL 上列举的经常用作 elicit 宾语的词

还有一次，我让同学们对一篇文章写个评论，有一个同学问：我想表达"这篇文章的论证非常充分"，该如何表达"充分"这个意义呢？

我们可以输入 argument，看一下和 argument 经常连用的形容词。从前 10 个词中，我们把表示消极意义的词排除掉，排除意义相差较远的 advanced 和 correct，再排除掉通常用来描述演绎论证的 valid 和 sound，剩下的 persuasive, convincing, compelling 就是最接近中文"充分"意思的词了。

	adjectives with argument	
1.	persuasive	argument is persuasive
2.	convincing	arguments convincing
3.	fallacious	argument is fallacious
4.	invalid	argument is invalid .
5.	valid	argument is valid
6.	compelling	argument is compelling
7.	sound	argument is sound
8.	advanced	argument is advanced
9.	false	argument is false
10.	correct	argument is correct
11.	weak	argument is weak
12.	irrelevant	argument is irrelevant
13.	simple	argument is simple
14.	relevant	argument is relevant
15.	similar	argument similar

图 9-7 和 argument 经常搭配的形容词

最后说个自己的例子。几年前，我写的一篇论文中有这么一句话：

> Given that it is probably not good pedagogy to show students plagiarism to be an easilyunderstood black-and-white issue, scholars suggested…

这句话想表达的意思是：剽窃未见得是个很容易理解的、非黑即白的问题，学者们由此给出了一些建议。文章提交后，审稿人建议我不要使用 black and white，原因是在当代英语中，black-

and-white 容易让人产生一些种族歧视的联想（即具有消极的联想意义）。后来我在 SKELL 上查了下 black-and-white，这个表达确实主要用来描述具体的事物，如照片、电影、电视等。在同事的建议下，我把 black and white 改成了 rigidly right or wrong。

	nouns modified by black-and-white	
1.	photograph	black-and-white photographs
2.	cinematography	black-and-white cinematography
3.	photography	black-and-white photography,
4.	photo	black-and-white photos
5.	illustration	black-and-white illustrations.
6.	print	black-and-white prints
7.	footage	black-and-white footage
8.	drawing	black-and-white drawings
9.	portrait	black-and-white portraits
10.	film	black-and-white film
11.	image	black-and-white images
12.	television	black-and-white television
13.	magazine	black-and-white magazine
14.	movie	black-and-white movie
15.	picture	black-and-white pictures

图 9-8　和 black-and-white 经常搭配的名词

4. 美国当代英语语料库

语料库，顾名思义，是汇集了众多真实语料的一个语言的仓库。美国当代英语语料库（Corpus of Contemporary American English，简称COCA）包含超过 10 亿词的文本，是目前最大的免费英语语料库之一。由于这个语料库每年都有扩充，其内容具有很好的时效性。

这个语料库中的文本细分为口语、小说、杂志、报纸、学术期刊等几大类型。通过观察一个词在不同类型中的分布,我们可以更容易了解一个词的语体特征。我们再把上例中的 black-and-white issue 输入检索栏,可以看到这样的说法并非完全不使用,但在学术语篇中仅出现了一次。

SECTION	ALL	BLOG	WEB	TV/M	SPOK	FIC	MAG	NEWS	ACAD
FREQ	26	3	3	5	4	0	4	6	1
WORDS (M)	993	128.6	124.3	128.1	126.1	118.3	126.1	121.7	119.8
PER MIL	0.03	0.02	0.02	0.04	0.03	0.00	0.03	0.05	0.01

图 9-9　COCA 语料库中 black-and-white issue 在不同语类中的使用情况

(三)句子的组织

Academic Phrasebank(https://www.phrasebank.manchester.ac.uk/)由曼彻斯特大学 John Morley 博士创建,是一个学术写作的词句模板库。如果你根据我们第三讲提到的"逆向工程法"理清了一篇论文的基本脉络,但真正落笔时,却不知如何表达,Academic Phrasebank 是一个很好的参考网站。

该网站横向的导航栏基于 John Swales 提出的"语步"概念,从介绍研究工作(Introducing work)、征引文献(Referring to sources)、描述方法(Describing methods)、汇报结果(Reporting results)、讨论结果(Discussing findings)和撰写结论(Writing

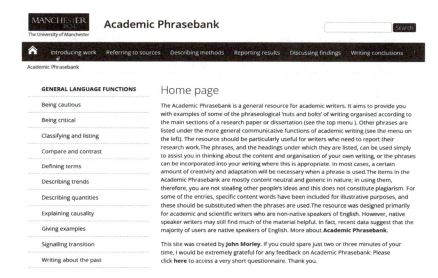

图 9-10 Academic Phrasebank 网站的主页

conclusions）六个方面为论文写作提供了丰富的写作短语和句型。

比如写到"讨论"部分的最后，你想给未来的研究提出建议，却不知如何措辞时，可以迅速定位到导航栏"讨论结果"下面的"给未来工作提供建议"，参考网站上提供的一些表达方式：

```
— Giving suggestions for future work
  This is an important issue for future research.
  Research questions that could be asked include …
  There are still many unanswered questions about …
  Several questions remain unanswered at present.
  Despite these promising results, questions remain.
  Further work is required to establish the viability of…
  Further research should be undertaken to investigate the …
  There is abundant room for further progress in determining …
  A further study with more focus on X is therefore suggested.
  Future studies on the current topic are therefore recommended.
  To develop a full picture of X, additional studies will be needed that …
  In future investigations, it might be possible to use a different X in which …
  Further studies, which take these variables into account, will need to be undertaken.
```

图 9-11 Academic Phrasebank 上有关"给未来工作提供建议"的语句

网站纵向的导航栏还提供了关于如何实现谨慎措辞（Being cautious）、如何进行学术批评（Being critical）、如何分类和列举（Classifying and listing）、如何比较和对比（Comparing and contrasting）等功能的语言资源。如从"比较和对比"导航栏中，我们可以学习到如何在一句话内做比较：

— Comparing within one sentence		
Oral societies tend to be more concerned with the present	whereas while	literate societies have a very definite awareness of the past.
Whereas While	oral societies tend to be more concerned with the present,	literate societies have a very definite awareness of the past.
This interpretation	differs from that contrasts with that is different from that	of Smith and Jones (2004) who argue that ….
In contrast to oral communities,		it is very difficult to get away from calendar time in literate societies.
Compared with people in oral cultures,		people in literate cultures organise their lives around clocks and calendars.

图 9-12　Academic Phrasebank 上提供的在一句话内"做比较"的例句

该网站给出的所有语言素材都来自英语母语者的学术论文。如果大家在平日的学习中，能逐步积累出一个自己所在学科和专业专属的 Phrasebank，一定会受益无穷。

（四）翻译工具

对写作学术论文是否应该使用翻译工具这个问题一直有些不同的声音。最近一些年，机器辅助翻译的质量不断提升，翻译软件确实能帮我们迅速地把想法转化成语言。因此，我个人觉得是可以利用的。

不过，翻译软件就像婴儿学步的"学步车"，需要"适度"利用。学术写作只是学术交流的一部分，学术交流还包括学术会议上的汇报和面对面的讨论。我们如果长时间依赖翻译软件，不利于培养出自己用另一门语言独立表达学术思想的能力。再者，虽然翻译软件大体可以帮我们把意思表达出来，但尚不能揣测出我们想要表达的信息重点，并把它们放在合理的位置上。

DeepL（https://www.deepl.com/translator）和谷歌翻译（https://translate.google.cn/）是目前翻译质量较高的两款翻译工具。我们不妨利用它们翻译一下上面的这段文字。

> However, translation software is like a toddler's 'walker' and needs to be used 'in moderation'. Academic writing is only one part of academic communication, which also includes presentations at academic conferences and face-to-face discussions. Relying on translation software for long periods of time is not conducive to developing the ability to express academic ideas independently in another language. Furthermore, while the translation software can generally help us get the meaning across, it cannot yet guess the focus of the message we want to convey and put it in the right place.

DeepL 给出的翻译

> However, translation software is like a toddler's "walker" and needs to be used "in moderation." Academic writing is only a part of academic communication, which also includes presentations at academic conferences and face-to-face discussions. If we rely on translation software for a long time, it is not conducive to cultivate our ability to express academic thoughts independently in another language. Furthermore, although translation software can generally help us express our meaning, it is not yet able to guess the key points of the information we want to express and put them in a reasonable place.

谷歌翻译给出的翻译

不难看出，目前翻译软件大体能将我们想表达的信息表达出来，翻译的准确性有一定的保证。不过人工复核与修改仍是利用翻译工具后不可缺省的环节。我们看翻译中间的一处：

原文：学术写作只是学术交流的一部分，学术交流还包括来自学术会议上的汇报和面对面的讨论。

Deep L：Academic writing is only one part of academic communication, which also includes presentations at academic conferences and face-to-face discussions.

谷歌翻译：Academic writing is only a part of academic communication, which also includes presentations at academic conferences and face-to-face discussions.

DeepL和谷歌翻译都把这句话翻译成了一个主从复合句,强调了主句中的信息,淡化了从句中的信息。可是,如果单看这句话,逗号分隔的两个小句地位相当,是并列的关系。如果从上下文来看,作者更强调的是从句中的信息。可见,在这句话的翻译中,机翻并没有很好地体会到我们想要表达的信息重点。

再如,两个翻译版本都用到了conducive一词,但用法并不一致,需要我们进一步查证。

(五)文献管理软件

文献的使用,主要关注的是如何通过有效引用,构建好的论证。事实上,文献使用还包括征引的一些技术细节,这些细节属于正确引用的范畴。

通常来讲,学术期刊对文内引用和文后引用有较为固定的格式要求。我们比较一下同一篇文章在不同引用格式下出现在文后引用(即参考文献)上的样子:

Flowerdew, J., & Li, Y. Y. (2007). Language re-use among Chinese apprentice scientists writing for publication. *Applied Linguistics, 28*(3), 440-465. doi:10.1093/applin/amm031 (APA格式)

Flowerdew, J., and Y. Y. Li. "Language Re-Use among Chinese Apprentice Scientists Writing for Publication." *Applied Linguistics* 28.3 (2007): 440-65.（MLA 格式）

可见，这些技术细节包括了一些引用要素出现的先后顺序，大小写、斜体/非斜体、标点等。如果我们手工录入一条参考文献，在这些细节处是很容易出错的。不少同学一想到参考文献就感到头疼，原因就在于此。

文献管理软件能帮我们把和写作相关的文献管理起来。更重要的是，它里面存储了一些通用的引用格式（如 APA, MLA, Chicago）和上千种期刊的特有引用格式。我们可以根据自己投稿期刊的要求，将文献管理软件上指定的文献以指定的格式自动插入文档之中，非常方便高效。

常见的文献管理软件有 Endnote, Mandeley, Zotero。不少写作者写作的全过程，包括下载文献、阅读文献、做笔记，都是在文献管理软件上完成的。

略作一句补充：文献管理软件并非万能，遇到一些特别的情况（比如不常见的文献类型，年代久远的文献，一些非英语的姓名拼写），还要多多发挥主观能动性，找到难题的解决方案。也建议大家手头常备一本自己学科最主流引用格式的手册。

最后，让我们回到开头的那个故事。金先生家那个三层工具箱是他的外公手工制作的。外公退休后，他的姨父奥伦继承了那个工具箱。可以想见，工具箱里的工具是在岁月中一件件添置的，也经历了岁月的筛选和检验。

因此,我们的工具箱里要有足够多的工具,但也要避免无限多。最终,实践会告诉你留下哪些,扔掉哪些。你也要爱惜它们,记得定时打理一下。

本讲练习

请尝试利用写作工具完善自己一篇论文的初稿。

第十讲　日　常

前面九讲和学术写作相关的方方面面，都可以归为写作技能的讨论。最后一讲，我们谈谈技能之外的东西。

（一）时间

没有时间是不写作的最好理由。曾几何时，在忙碌的生活中，我也总希望能找到属于自己的"大块"时间用以写作，然而屡屡在现实面前败下阵来。直到一日，看到查尔斯·布考斯基（Charles Bukowski）① 的小诗《空气、光线、时间和空间》②。

> "-you know, I've either had a family, a job,
>
> something has always been in the way
>
> but now
>
> I've sold my house, I've found this

---

① BUKOWSKI C. The last night of the earth poems [M]. New York: Ecco, 2002.
② 配诗的漫画很可爱，请见 https://www.themarginalian.org/2013/10/04/charles-bukowski-air-and-light-and-time-and-space/[2022-11-05]

place, a large studio, you should see the space and
the light.
for the first time in my life, I'm going to have
a place and the time to
create."

no baby, if you're going to create
you're going to create whether you work
16 hours a day in a coal mine
or
you're going to create in a small room with 3 children
while you're on
welfare,

you're going to create with part of your mind and your body
blown away,
you're going to create blind
crippled
demented,
you're going to create with a cat crawling up your
back while
the whole city trembles in earthquake, bombardment,
flood and fire.

baby, air and light and time and space

have nothing to do with it

and don't create anything

except maybe a longer life to find

new excuses

for.

我们总在等待万事俱备、可以全心投入写作的时刻。查尔斯告诉我们：理想的写作条件可能根本不存在。

海伦·索德（Helen Sword）教授在《成功的学者如何写作》一书中对成功的学者有这样一番描述：

Successful writers carve out time and space for their writing in a striking variety of ways, but they all do it somehow.[①]

请大家注意 carve out 这个短语，carve 的意思不是"找到"，也不是"挤出"，而是"切割"，比如 carve out a pumpkin 是切掉南瓜上的一部分，用以制作万圣节的南瓜灯。因此，在海伦教授看来，成功的学者不是在寻找写作的时间，而是把属于写作的时间"切割"出来，不作他用。

---

① SWORD H. Air & light & time & space: How successful academics write [M]. Boston: Harvard University Press, 2017: 4.

《如何文思泉涌》的作者保罗·席尔瓦（Paul J. Silvia）也表达了非常相似的观点：

Instead of finding time to write, allot time to write.[①]

allot 同 carve out 的内涵相似，就像我们需要给吃饭、睡觉安排时间一样，也需要给写作计划、安排固定的时间。

很多优秀的写作者都十年如一日地写作。从《加西亚·马尔克斯访谈录》里，我们得知马尔克斯在许多年里每天从上午九点写到下午两、三点，因为他相信"写作是通过写作学会的"[②]。从《我的职业是小说家》里，我们得知村上春树"清晨起床，每天五到六小时集中心力执笔写稿"，三十年如一日。他说："要让惯性的轮子以一定的速度准确无误地旋转起来，对待持之以恒，何等

[①] SILVA P J. How to write a lot: A practical guide to productive academic writing [M]. Second Edition. New York: American Psychological Association, 2018: 12.

[②] 吉恩·贝尔-维尔达. 加西亚·马尔克斯访谈录 [G]. 许志强, 译. 南京：南京大学出版社, 2019: 19.

小心翼翼也不为过。"①

村上所说的小心翼翼，我自己深有体会。生活中有太多的事情会打乱我们日日如一的节奏。在保证基本作息的前提下，一天中哪一个小段的时间最不容易被打扰，最有可能专心投入写作呢？我想我们不妨拿自己做个实验，选定几个时间段，分别尝试一段时间②。

（二）写作灵感

当我们终于每日为写作"切割"出了一小段时间，下一个问题又来了：我没有状态，也没有灵感，写不出来。

罗伯特·博伊斯（Robert Boice）教授在《作为写作者的教授们》一书中汇报了自己的一项实验③。他把一些有写作困难的大学教授随机分成三组。第一组非必要不得写作；第二组计划了50次的写作，灵感来了就写，没有就不写；第三组同样计划了50次的写作，但每一次都必须完成（如果他们某次没写，惩罚措施是向自己不喜欢的组织寄一张支票）。图10-1为我们呈现了三组教授实验结束时的表现：从写作产出来看，第三组每天完成的页数是第二组的3.5倍，第一组的16倍。换言之，如果依靠写作灵感，

---

① 村上春树. 我的职业是小说家［M］. 施小炜，译. 海口：南海出版公司，2017：129.
② 我实践的结果是清晨，每天的5：00-7：00成了我的"写作时间"。清晨起来，经历了一宿的睡眠，脑子尚未被任何日常杂事所占据，能够比较快地进入和保持专心致志的状态。选定好时间，剩下的就是日复一日了，其中的"日"，包括寒暑假，包括周末，也包括节日。
③ BOICE R. Professors as writers: A self-help guide to productive writing［M］. Stillwater, OK: New Forums Press, 1990：79-80.

我们的写作产量仅比完全不写好一点点。

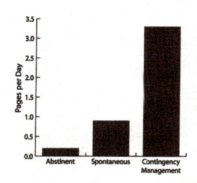

图 10-1　三组教授的每日写作产量

博伊斯对三组教授的实验，还有一个更重要的发现：第三组的参与者平均每一天就能产生一个好想法，而第二组需要两天，第一组需要五天（见图 10-2），用他的话说：好想法是从写作中来的（Writing breeds good ideas for writing）。

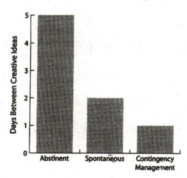

图 10-2　三组教授产生好想法的时间间隔

这个研究发现为有规律写作的益处提供了最好的证据。这一益处或许可以这样解释：当我们保持了规律写作的状态，潜意识便会持续不断地为我们工作，好想法便会源源不断地"冒"出来。

（三）完成度与精度

写作的时间设定好了，也按部就班，不那么寄望灵光一现的时刻了，可是写作进展缓慢、总是半途而废怎么办呢？

我们的头脑很难同时处理很多事情。如果想着写作内容的同时，还思考用词是否得当、精练，句子中信息的位置安排是否合理，句子之间的衔接是否自然、流畅等，那我们文章可能推进得很缓慢，也容易半途而废。因此，我觉得先求完成度，再求精度，是开启学术写作的正确方式。

小说家斯蒂芬·金在《写作这回事》里提出"闭门写作，开门修改"的理念，还有学者在写作时严格分割写作和修改的时间，这些都是首先追求完成度的表现。追求完成度，需要我们暂时放下追求完美的心。初稿一定是不完美的，我们要从心理上接受这件事。

"完成"的标志是什么呢？就是把头脑中的想法落实到了纸面，形成了文字。以学术论文为例，当它有了完整的结构，也有了清晰的论证逻辑时，我们就可以说它"完成"了。至于语法是不是全部正确、动词的选用是不是有活力，句子里有没有一些冗余的成分，句式有没有一定的变化和节奏，句子之间是否有很好的衔接，这些可能都不是在"追求完成"这个阶段需要考虑的事情。

美国作家安·拉莫特在《关于写作：一只鸟接着一只鸟》这

本书里，给我们讲了一个她童年的故事。

三十年前，我的哥哥十岁，第二天得交一篇鸟类报告。虽然他之前有三个月的时间写这份作业，却一直没有进展。当时在我家位于博利纳斯的度假小屋，他坐在餐桌前，周围散置着作业簿、铅笔和一本本未打开的鸟类书籍。它面对眼前的艰巨任务，不知如何着手，简直快哭出来了。后来我父亲在他身边坐下，把手放在他肩上说："一只鸟接着一只鸟，伙伴。只要一只鸟接着一只鸟，按部就班地写。"[①]

是的，当我们不知道怎么写的时候，最好的办法，就是直接开写。以实证研究论文为例，研究既然是我们亲自完成的，那一定用到了某些材料或设备，可以就此写一小段；在收集数据时，一定是按照时间步步展开的，可以就研究过程写一小段；一定是得到了某些结果的，可以就主要的研究发现描述一番。

从一个字、一个词、一个句子、一个段落开始，哪怕写得很糟糕，都没有关系。只要开始了第一步，就会有第二步、第三步。只要写了出来，不管写得多差，我们都还有机会把它改好。

改好的过程是对精度的追求，我们希望落在纸面的语言能更准确、流畅、有逻辑。我们可从别人已经发表的文字中借鉴经验；可以多和导师、师兄师姐沟通，请他们帮忙提出建议；也可以多

[①] 安·拉莫特. 关于写作：一只鸟接着一只鸟 [M]. 朱耘, 译. 北京：商务印书馆, 2013：41-42.

多参会,从别人提出的问题中进一步完善自己的文章。

与此同时,我们是最了解自己论文的人。在完成的基础上,我们可以把自己化身为一个严苛的读者,与那个写作的自我拉开一定的距离。修改自己的文章无疑伴随着痛苦,因为这个过程包含了一次次的自我否定。然而可以修改也是写作的优势。事实上,修改可以一直进行下去。需要提醒的是,到了修改的某个阶段,要给自己按下暂停键。

(四)语言习惯

日常和人交往时,我们会感到有的人说话"没逻辑"或是"只说半截儿",我们自己有时也会觉得和别人说的话"词不达意"。可见学术语言,说到底,不是某种凌驾于生活之上的语言。既然都是为更好地交流思想,学术语言和生活中的语言对准确、简练、逻辑的追求大概只有程度的分别而已。因此,我们在日常生活中,要培养好的语言习惯。

在叶圣陶先生看来,良好的语言习惯是:"无论何时不说一句不完整的话,说一句话一定要表达出一个意思,使人家听了都能够明白;无论何时不把一个不很了解的词硬用在语言里,也不把一个不很适当的词强凑在语言里。我们还要求自己,无论何时不乱用一个连词,不多用或者少用一个助词。说一句话,一定要在应当'然而'的地方才'然而',应当'那么'的地方才'那么',需要'吗'的地方不缺少'吗',不需要'了'的地方不无谓地'了'。"①

培养好的语言习惯，就在生活的点滴。社团招新时，试着清晰地介绍自己；同学因病缺席了一堂课，主动为他复述老师上课的内容；和导师每周见面，概括而简练地汇报自己一周的学习进展。

尝试、反思、进步、累积，会最终作用到我们生活的方方面面，包括写作。

（五）学术批评

除了上述行为习惯，学术写作也是对众多情感品质的锤炼，其中最重要的就是如何看待学术批评。

学术写作的产物，说到底，不是用来自我玩赏的。我们希望自己的新观点、新发现、新成果能得以传播、推动学术共同体的发展。在得以传播之前，学术"守门人"，也就是审稿人会严格把关我们的学术文章。如果我们的文章没有达到一定的学术水准，会被拒稿。席尔瓦教授把我们要投稿的学术论文比作海龟的幼崽，从巢窝到大海的一路并非坦途②。

很多学科一些好期刊的接收率都在 10% 左右。如何面对拒稿，应该是所有学术新人的必修课。我想用《终身成长》里面提到的两种心智对应对待拒稿的两种态度。拥有固定型心智的人倾向于

---

① 叶圣陶. 怎样写作 [M]. 北京：中华书局，2007：57.

② SILVA P J. How to write a lot: A practical guide to productive academic writing [M]. Second Edition. New York: American Psychological Association, 2018: 93.

将拒稿视作对自身能力的否定,进而生发出"我的努力都白费了"或者"我不适合做学术"之类的想法;而拥有成长性心智的人会更积极地看待他人的批评性意见,找出其中具有建设性的部分,进而把拒稿当作成长的机遇,进一步锤炼自己的能力。①

看过一则新闻:密歇根州立大学地球与环境科学博士生凯特琳·柯比(Caitlin Kirby)穿着自己用17封拒信做成的裙子参加博士论文的答辩。柯比自嘲地说:自己收到的拒信远不止这些,做完裙子还剩很多。②

柯比脸上自信的笑容,体现的就是这种成长型心智。当我们收到拒稿信时,往往也会收到文章不能发表的理由。这些理由和意见对我们都是极有价值的信息。评审意见中的批评不一定全部

---

① 卡罗尔·德韦克. 终身成长:重新定义成功的思维模式 [M]. 楚祎楠,译. 南昌:江西人民出版社,2017:7-8.

② STRUAN J. Grad student defended her dissertation while wearing a skirt made of rejection letters [EB/OL]. (2010-10-17) [2022-11-06] https://www.sohu.com/a/473980954_121124320

正确，但思考和辨析这些批评具有非凡的意义和价值。

成长型心智模式并非刻在每个人的基因里，而是在岁月中锻造出来的。下次看见躺在电子邮件中的拒稿信时，请将那个"My paper is rejected"的想法逐出脑海，用下面这个新的措辞取代它：

My paper is yet to be published.

（六）底层品质

学术写作技巧的背后，是一些本质、稳定、底层的东西。比如，第一讲我们讲了读者意识。读者意识的底层，是同理心。在日常总能考虑到别人的关切和需要的人，可能会更容易在心中给读者留下位置。再如，第二讲我们谈了论证。论证能力的底层，是问题意识。论证，说到底，是由尚未解决的问题驱动的。而问题意识的底层，是好奇心。

和一般的写作不同，学术写作通常承载着一个沉甸甸的研究。科学研究是以求真为目标的。几年前，我和几位大二的学生采访了中国科学院生物物理研究所的陈畅研究员。谈及学问之道，她用了"通透"一词。她说：我们追求真理，不仅仅是工作上求真，做人、生活都应该是真实的一个状态。

有人说：You are what you write。我同意这样的说法。但我更喜欢的说法是：You become what you write。学术写作体现着我们那些本质、稳定、底层的东西，也在漫长的岁月中塑造和磨砺着我们，让我们成为更好的人。

我们一起来读读苏东坡的《观潮》。

　　庐山烟雨浙江潮，
　　未至千般恨不消。
　　到得还来别无事，
　　庐山烟雨浙江潮。

学术写作，对很多人来说，充满了"庐山烟雨浙江潮"般的神秘。当文章屡屡被拒，可能会升起不消的千般遗憾。不过终有一日，当你像大厨一样掌握了烹饪的秘方，文章终于发表在心仪的期刊，被别人问及感受时，你可能会说一句：其实还好啦。

终于得见"庐山烟雨浙江潮"的美景时，我们一定不是惊喜，不是狂喜，而是淡淡的欢喜。

因为，所有必经的路途，包括弯路，我们都一步步地走过了。

本讲最后，和大家分享一个学生在课后写下的文字。感恩这段和大家共同探讨学术写作的时光。

附：

棉花糖在路上

20世纪60年代，斯坦福大学心理学家沃尔特·米歇尔设计了世界上最著名的社会学实验之一——棉花糖实验（the Marshmallow Test）。实验中，四岁左右的幼童被独自放在一个房间里。研究者把一颗棉花糖放到他面前，并在离开房间前告诉他，如果可以等待15分钟不吃，就可以得到双倍返还。事实上，告诉一个四岁的孩子要等15分钟才能享用他所喜爱的食物，就如同告诉成年人，您的三分糖加冰奶茶前面还有110单，预估将在三小时后开始为您制作，请耐心等待。

当研究者离开后，三分之二的孩子选择吃掉了棉花糖。这当中，有的孩子其实已经等待了十四分半，但最终还是没能坚持下去。而有趣的是，三分之一的孩子做到了。在等待过程中，他们内心极度挣扎，或是将棉花糖拿起来又放回去，或是在房间里焦躁地踱步，或是不停拉扯他们的裙子或裤子。这些孩子，虽年仅四岁，却似乎已经懂得了成功最重要的法则——延迟满足。

看着孩子们抓耳挠腮、坐立难安的小模样，我一时感到心疼，而后想来又觉得，做研究、写论文的过程难道不是与他们颇为相似，甚至难度还要略胜一筹的吗？学术写作与棉花糖实验一样，同时需要专注与毅力，研究者像实验中的孩子们一样伏案独坐，每天集中三四个小时的意识执笔写作,坚持半年、一年甚至两年往上。如果借用村上春树的比喻,学术写作更近于一种体力劳动,和长跑颇为相像。

而相比于棉花糖实验,做科研、写论文的独特难度在于:实验中,"延迟"的时间被固定为15分钟,且所有接受"延迟"孩子在实验结束后都立刻得到了两块棉花糖的"满足",前者是后者的充分条件。而学术写作则大为不同,一方面,其"延迟"没有固定的期限,它像是一门手艺活,从定题目、找素材、列提纲,到初稿、二稿、三稿,每一步都是"如切如磋,如琢如磨"的过程。而另一方面,即使历经"延迟","棉花糖"也未必能到来。辛苦构思撰写、反复打磨了好久的论文,最终却接到了一纸冰冷的退稿通知,这样的经历想必许多研究人员都不陌生,甚至有人发明出了"常态化退稿"一词来聊表安慰。因此,在学术写作中,"延迟"可能仅为"棉花糖"的必要条件。

那既然"棉花糖"的到来不是现在,也不是未来的一年之内,甚至可能永远都不会到来,那从事研究的人为什么还要像打磨一件艺术品一样坚持学术写作呢?自幼爱好声乐、研一起便加入国科大博士合唱团的我,似乎在这一点上有些许的感悟和理解。团里许多小伙伴的培养单位在京外所,但即使在合唱团的时间极其有限,他们也出于近乎纯粹的热爱而提高声乐,从不偷工减料。他们似乎想得很简单,只想保持好当下的乐感和声乐练习的节奏,不那么在乎以后,在乎成本和收益,在乎"棉花糖"。相似地,每位研究者在写作过程中,固然也有自己的局限性,可学术写作的魅力似乎也正在于此：我们渐渐学会了与"唯结果论"相抗衡，并开始将如何成长、如何快乐、如何掌握更好的节奏、找到更适合自己的方向视作我们永恒的主题。

科研与学术写作这项职业，似乎应当是无所谓胜负成败的。论文发表的刊物、得奖与否、被引量的高低，这些或许是历经"延迟"后的"棉花糖"，却不能成为本质问题。写出来的文字是否真正反映了自己的科研实践、达到了内心设定的标准才至为重要。在这层意义上，学术写作确实与村上所比喻的马拉松有共通之处：对于论文作者而言，其写作动机应该是对拓展人类知识边界的渴望，应是安静的、内驱的、纯粹的。而日复一日地坚持写作，既是想在不断突破极限的过程中发掘灵感，也是想跟学术写作想成为朋友，成为亲人，成为恋人。想让大脑成为写作的一部分，或是让写作成为身体的一部分，是手和脚，或者眼睛，或者鼻子。

执笔于此，乍然忆起杜垚老师课中为我们展示的王阳明《传习录》中的一句，遂即动笔将原有题目"忘掉棉花糖"改为了"棉花糖在路上"："立志用功如种树然，方其根芽，犹未有干，及其有干，尚未有枝，枝而后叶，叶而后花实。初种根时，只管栽培灌溉，勿作枝想，勿作叶想，勿作花想，勿作实想。悬想何益，但不忘栽培之功，怕没有枝叶花实？"当前的我们在学术写作领域犹处于"初种根时"，正是坚忍又疯狂地累积营养的时期。因此眼下不必焦虑那些掌控不了的未来，"勿作花想，勿作实想"，只管默默地花时间积累写作的"延迟"，持之以恒，不乱节奏。只要日日动笔，总会产生出某些类似观念的东西出来。悬想何益！但有"延迟"之功，还怕没有"棉花糖"之实？棉花糖在路上。

金秋（中国科学院大学 2020 级研究生）

参考答案

第一讲

练习 1

第一个选段来自马丁·塞林格曼 2011 年发表的专著，目标读者是公众和一般心理学爱好者。

SELIGMAN M. Flourish: A visionary new understanding of happiness and well-being [M]. New York: Simon & Schuster, 2011.

第二个选段来自马丁·塞林格曼于同年发表的一篇期刊文章，目标读者是心理学同行。

FORGEARD M, JAYAWICKREME E, KERN M, SELIGMAN M. Doing the right thing: Measuring wellbeing for public policy [J]. International Journal of Wellbeing, 2011, 1(1): 79-106.

两个选段都向读者说明了幸福理论中 Happiness 一词被替换成 Well-being 的原因。两个选段均给出了这一替换的背景，即作者十年前幸福理论的主要内容。所不同的是，第二个选段假设读者具备相关的背景知识，行文中对这一理论只有扼要的介绍；而第一个选段假设读者不具备相关的背景知识，不仅介绍了幸福理论中三个主要元素的定义，说明了元素之间的联系和区别（如"积极情绪"和"心流"的关系），还给出了一些个性化的例子（如作者自己打桥牌的例子），帮助读者更好地理解这一理论中的重要内容。

此外，两个选段均提出了 Happiness 和 Well-being 的区别。所不同的是，第二个选段对两者区别的阐释只有一句话（第二段第二行的目的性小句）；而第一个选段为了更好地说明"Well-being is a construct"中"construct"的意义，举出了气象学中"天气"（weather）和政治学中"自由"这两个概念做类比，帮助读者从日常生活更为熟悉的话题中，理解 Well-being 的构念特征。

再者，作者在第二个选段用通俗易懂的方式向读者解释了 operationalize 这一专业术语的意思；在解释 Well-being 这一构念中各要素的测量方式时，也避免了使用 subjective 和 objective，而只是笼统地指出"它们不是仅仅基于你感到有多少积极情绪、有多投入、有多大意义感的自陈式的报告"。

练习 2

一、内容方面：

（1）关于提升幸福感的 5 个小练习：作者在选段一中概括地介绍了这 5 个小练习；选段二中，对效果最好的 3 个练习（"The Gratitude Visit""Three Blessings""Signature Strength"）有非常详尽的介绍。

（2）选段一对通过网络收取数据的优势和弱点有辩证的思考，选段二未包含这样的思考。

（3）选段一对实验参与者的人数、性别、年龄、受教育程度、收入、种族等信息均有介绍；选段二只介绍了参与实验的人数。

（4）选段一对实验设计中的一些细节有所介绍，如实验持续的时间（6 个月）、参与实验的激励机制、对实验者的邮件提醒等；

选段二没有此类细节信息的介绍。

二、语言方面：

（一）时间词的使用：

选段一有 9 处时间词的使用：

1. Each exercise was delivered via the Internet and could be completed *within one week*.

2. We followed our participants *for six months*, periodically measuring symptoms of both depression and happiness.

3. *Over the course of approximately one month*, we recruited 577 adult participants…

4. *After* participants agreed to the terms presented, they answered a series of basic demographic questions and completed two questionnaires, …

5. *Then* participants received a randomly assigned exercise.

6. They were instructed to return to the Web site to complete follow-up questionnaires *after* completing their assigned exercise.

7. The first reminder, sent *early in the week*, repeated the instructions for their assigned exercise.

8. The second reminder e-mail, sent *later in the week*, reminded participants to return to the Web site for the follow-up questionnaires…

9. When participants returned to the Web site *after* performing their exercise, they completed the same measures of happiness and depression administered at pretest.

选段二有 3 处时间词的使用：

1. **First** they take depression and happiness tests, such as the Center for Epidemiological Studies depression scale and the authentic happiness inventory, which are both on www.authentichappiness.org.

2. **Next** we randomly assign them to a single exercise that is either active or a placebo.

3. All exercises require two to three hours **over the course of one week**.

（二） 意图性小句：

选段一有 4 处意图性/原因性小句的使用，交代了作者实验设计背后的用意：

1. At this stage in our intervention research, this convenience sample served our purposes well, **because** on average we have 300 new registrants every day to our Web site (www.authentichappiness.org), which contains many of the positive questionnaires for free.

2. **On the basis of** these considerations, we chose to use the Internet.

3. **In order to** ensure good follow-up, we did tell participants, however, that upon completion of follow-up tests at one week, one month, three months, and six months after completing the exercise, they would be entered into a lottery.

4. In addition, participants answered a manipulation check question **to assess** whether they had in fact completed the exercise as instructed

during the relevant time period (scored *yes* or *no*).

选段二无意图性/原因性小句的使用。

(三) 人称代词：

在选段一的 56 个句子中，有 29 处使用了第一人称代词（we/our），未使用第二人称代词，有 14 处使用了第三人称代词（they）；在选段二的 69 个句子中，有 14 处使用了第一人称代词（we/our），有 79 处使用了第二人称代词（you/your/yours/yourself），第二人称的使用极大地拉近了作者与读者的距离，有 3 处使用了第三人称代词（they）。

(四) 语态：

在选段一的 56 个句子中，共有 15 句使用了被动语态，其余均为主动语态；在选段二的 69 个句子中，仅有 3 句使用了被动语态，其余均为主动语态。被动语态的使用一定程度上"增加"了实验的客观色彩。

(五) 选词：

相比于选段二，选段一的选词更为正式、专业。例如：

Participants were asked to write down three things that went well each day and their causes every night for one week. In addition, they were asked to provide a causal explanation for each good thing.（选段一）

Every night for the next week, set aside ten minutes before you go to sleep. Write down three things that went well today and why they went well.（选段二）

For our first large RCT, we designed five happiness exercises and one placebo control exercise. (选段一)

In our first web study, we tried six exercises. (选段二)

练习3

作者：庞泰然（中国科学院大学 2021 级博士研究生）

文献信息：

XIAO S, CHEN C, XIA Q, et al. Lightweight, strong, moldable wood via cell wall engineering as a sustainable structural material [J]. Science, 2021, 374, 465-471, https://doi.org/10.1126/science.abg9556.

LI Z, CHEN C, MI R, et al. A strong, tough, and scalable structural material from fast-growing bamboo [J]. Advanced Materials, 2020, 32, 1906308, https://doi.org/10.1002/adma.201906308.

第一篇论文来自《科学》；第二篇论文来自材料科学领域的顶级期刊《先进材料》。两篇文章来自同一个研究团队。我将以两篇论文的摘要为例，从读者意识的角度，分析两篇摘要的异同。

摘要一

Wood is a sustainable structural material, but it cannot be easily shaped while maintaining its mechanical properties. We report a processing strategy that uses cell wall engineering to shape flat sheets of hardwood into versatile three-dimensional (3D) structures. After breaking down wood's lignin component and closing the vessels and fibers by evaporating water, we partially re-swell the wood in a rapid water-shock process that selectively opens the vessels. This forms a distinct wrinkled cell wall structure that allows the material to be folded and molded into desired shapes. The resulting 3D-molded wood is six times stronger than the starting wood and comparable to widely used lightweight materials such as aluminum alloys. This approach widens wood's potential as a structural material, with lower environmental impact for buildings and transportation applications.

摘要二

Lightweight structural materials with high strength are desirable for advanced applications in transportation, construction, automotive, and aerospace. Bamboo is one of the fastest growing plants with a peak growth rate up to 100 cm per day. Here, a simple and effective top-down approach is designed for processing natural bamboo into a lightweight yet strong bulk structural material with a record high tensile strength of $\approx$ 1 GPa and toughness of 9.74 MJ m^{-3}. More specifically, bamboo is densified by the partial removal of its lignin and hemicellulose, followed by hot-pressing. Long, aligned cellulose

> nanofibrils with dramatically increased hydrogen bonds and largely reduced structural defects in the densified bamboo structure contribute to its high mechanical tensile strength, flexural strength, and toughness. The low density of lignocellulose in the densified bamboo leads to a specific strength of 777 MPa cm^3 g^{-1}, which is significantly greater than other reported bamboo materials and most structural materials (e.g., natural polymers, plastics, steels, and alloys). This work demonstrates a potential large-scale production of lightweight, strong bulk structural materials from abundant, fast-growing, and sustainable bamboo.

摘要一描述了一种利用常见木质纤维素生物质原料制备高性能材料的方法，摘要二则描述了同样基于木质纤维素生物质原料的一种高机械强度材料的生产。摘要一和摘要二均在开头简单介绍研究背景后对实验过程进行了阐述，并在结尾处展望了所得产品的应用前景。

仔细对比两篇摘要，我发现了以下几点不同。

第一，相较于摘要一，摘要二在实验过程的论述中加入了少量对实验机理的阐述，而摘要一更多是对实验过程的描述。

第二，两篇摘要均对所得到材料的性能进行了描述，相比于摘要一，摘要二给出了一些实验所得的数据。比如，第三句句末的"tensile strength of ≈1 GPa and toughness of 9.74 MJ m^{-3}"凸显了所制备材料的优异性能。

第三，在语言方面，摘要二更多地使用了被动语态、专业术语和名词短语。例如，摘要二使用了"high mechanical tensile strength""flexural strength""toughness"等专业术语。再如，摘要二第四句对"去除木质素……"的相关描述中，使用了名词短语"the partial removal of its lignin"；而摘要一则使用了动词短语"breaking down wood's lignin component"。

上述差异和两本期刊面对的读者群体不同有关。《科学》面向更多非专业领域的读者，因此摘要一应深入浅出地介绍论文的内容并尽可能地抓住读者的眼球，句式以主动句为主，用词专业性不强。《先进材料》主要面向本领域的研究人员，因此摘要二需着重强调论文成果在本领域内的先进性从而凸显该工作的重要意义，在语言表达方面更显客观、抽象、凝练，用词专业程度强。针对不同的读者群体选择合适的内容、词语、句式有利于我们的文章更好地被读者理解。

第二讲

练习 1

（1）这是一个演绎论证。论证的前提为：没有图或没有对话的书没有用（大前提），我姐姐的书没有图和对话（小前提）；结论为：我姐姐的这本书是没有用的。这个演绎论证是一个有效论证，但并非可靠论证。大前提不为真，因为存在没有图或对话但依然有用的书；小前提可能为真，也可能为假（爱丽丝只是瞄了几眼，我们无从知道整本书是不是有图书或插图）。由于存在假的前提，那么这个论证的结论为假。这个论证不是一个可靠的论证。

（2）这是一个类比论证。论证的前提是：下一次从楼梯或房子坠落和这一次坠落兔子洞有很多相似之处，这一次坠落我没有受伤；结论为：下一次坠落我也不会受伤。这个论证不是一个高质量的类比论证，因为两次坠落的情形可能完全不同。

（3）这是一个演绎论证。前提是：如果我吃了蛋糕后变大，那么我能拿到钥匙（从而离开房间），如果我吃了蛋糕后变小，那么我能爬过门缝（从而离开房间），我或者变大，或者变小；结论是：我能离开房间。这个演绎论证是有问题的，因为她未考虑到吃了蛋糕既不会变大也不会变小的一种可能性。事实上，身体保持原状的可能性极大，如她立即发现：She ate a little bit, and said anxiously to herself "Which way? Which way?" holding her hand on the top of her head to feel which way it was growing; and she was quite surprised to find that she remained the same size.

（4）这是一个演绎论证。论证的前提为：蛇会吃蛋（大前提），爱丽丝吃蛋（小前提）；结论是：爱丽丝是蛇。这是一个无效论证（中项不周延）。后被爱丽丝反驳后，蛇修改了大前提：不管是什么，只要吃蛋就是蛇。虽然经过修改这个论证变成了一个有效论证，但它不是一个可靠论证，因为我们很容易举出吃蛋但不是蛇的反例。

练习 2

（1）选段一的核心观点是：人类对现实中可怕森林大火的无动于衷令人感到悲伤。作者是通过类比的方式得出这一观点的。作者论证的前提是：《小鹿斑比》中的烧死斑比妈妈的森林大火和今年夏天的森林大火有诸多相似之处；电影制作人对大火带来的死亡和悲伤的无视令人不快；结论是：人类对现实中可怕森林大火的无动于衷令人感到悲伤。

（2）选段二的观点是：《小鹿斑比》电影如实反映了森林大火对生态的影响，但选段一存在以"非黑即白"的视角看待自然现象的逻辑谬误。

练习 3

作者：鲁运（中国科学院半导体研究所 2021 级博士生）

这篇论文①从磁电响应的角度建立了斯格明子的一个通用模型。下面的选段来自文章的摘要部分，体现了很好的论证逻辑。

> We develop a general theory to classify magnetic skyrmions and related spin textures in terms of their magnetoelectric multipoles. Since magnetic skyrmions are now established in insulating materials, where the magnetoelectric multipoles govern the linear magnetoelectric response, our classification provides a recipe for manipulating the magnetic properties of skyrmions using applied electric fields. We apply our formalism to skyrmions and antiskyrmions of different helicities, as well as to magnetic bimerons, which are topologically, but not geometrically, equivalent to skyrmions. We show that the nonzero components of the magnetoelectric multipole and magnetoelectric response tensors are uniquely determined by the topology, helicity, and geometry of the spin texture. Therefore, we propose straightforward linear magnetoelectric response measurements as an alternative to Lorentz microscopy for characterizing insulating skyrmionic textures.

摘要开篇，作者提出全文最主要的贡献：建立斯格明子的一个通用模型。这个贡献也是全文的结论，是通过归纳论证，而且

---

① BHOWAL S, SPALDIN N A. Magnetoelectric classification of skyrmions [J]. Physical Review Letters, 2022, 128, 227204.

是完全归纳论证得出的。其中的论证逻辑为:

前提 1a: 我们提出的模型能解释磁斯格明子家族里的布洛赫型;

前提 1b: 我们提出的模型能解释磁斯格明子家族里的尼尔型;

前提 1c: 我们提出的模型能解释磁斯格明子家族里的双半子;

前提 2: 磁斯格明子家族里有且仅有布洛赫型、尼尔型和双半子;

结论: 我们提出的模型对于磁斯格明子家族具有普适性。

可简化为:

前提 1: B 理论能够解释 a, b, c;
前提 2: A 的所有成员为 a, b, c;
结论: B 理论对于 A 是普适的。

接下来,作者阐述了他们想到用磁电响应来建立理论的原因。其中的论证逻辑为:

前提 1: 电可控磁;
前提 2: 磁斯格明子可以存在于一个良好的电调控环

境中；

  结论：可以尝试用电来调控磁斯格明子。

可简化为：

  前提 1：A 可以调控 B；
  前提 2：C 在 B 中；
  结论：A 可以调控 C。

最后，作者提出了表征的新方案。其中的论证逻辑为：

  前提 1：斯格明子的指纹特征或指标有拓扑数、螺旋度、自旋纹理的几何图样；
  前提 2：磁电响应张量的非零分量由上述特征唯一确定；
  结论：可以通过线性磁电响应测量作为另一种斯格明子的表征方法。

可简化为：

  前提 1：A 有特征 B；
  前提 2：B 可以唯一得出一个 C；
  结论：可以用 C 来表征 A。

第三讲

练习 1

作者：黄昕怡（中国科学院大学 2022 级硕士生）

学术论文讨论分析
——以《自然》上的一篇论文①为例

1. 段落分析

<u>In summary</u>, <u>the current results indicate that</u> the development of infants later diagnosed with ASD differs from that of their typical peers by 2–6 months of age.¹ <u>These results</u>, while still limited in sample size, document the derailment of skills that would otherwise guide typical socialization, and this early divergence from normative experience <u>suggests</u> a means by which diverse genetic liabilities are instantiated, developmentally, into a spectrum of affectedness.² Given the interdependence of individual experience with brain structure and function, and with gene expression and methylation, <u>these results suggest</u> how a single individual's outcome will be	讨论包含两个段落。 首段总结了本研究的结果，并给出了一些可能的解释。 首段首句高度总结了本研究的最主要结果（In summary, ... results indicate...）。 随后，第二句和第三句逐步递进，对该结果分别给出了发育和基因层面的解释和推论（suggest）。

---

① JONES W, KLIN A. Attention to eyes is present but in decline in 2–6-month-old infants later diagnosed with autism [J]. Nature, 2013, 504, 427–431. https://doi.org/10.1038/nature12715.

shaped not only by initial genotypic vulnerabilities, but also by the atypical experiences that arise as a consequence of those vulnerabilities, instantiating a wide spectrum of affectedness.³	
In children later diagnosed with ASD, eye looking shows mean decline by at least 2 months.⁴ To our surprise, however, those early levels of eye looking appear to begin at normative levels.⁵ This contradicts prior hypotheses of a congenital absence of social adaptive orientation and suggests instead that some social-adaptive behaviors may initially be intact in newborns later diagnosed with ASD.⁶ If confirmed in larger samples, this would offer a remarkable opportunity for treatment: predispositions that are initially intact suggest a neural foundation that might be built upon, offering far more positive possibilities than if that foundation were absent from the outset.⁷ Equally exciting, these data fit well within the framework of long-studied animal models of the neural systems subserving filial orientation and attachment: they highlight a narrow period for future investigation, spanning the transition from experience-expectant to experience-dependent mechanisms.⁸ A critical next step will be to measure densely sampled developmental change in gene expression and brain growth, in tandem with detailed quantification of behaviour; in short, measuring gene-brain behaviour growth charts of infant social engagement to understand the developmental pathogenesis of social disability.⁹	讨论第二段从意义、不足、展望等多角度展开。 首先呼应了引言中提出的研究问题。 第六句将本研究与现有理论关联（contradict）。 进而指出本研究的局限和意义（if…, this would offer a remarkable opportunity for…）， 第八句从不同的角度将本研究与现有研究关联（fit well within…）。 最后是后续研究方向的展望（a critical next step will be…）。

2. 写作思路

这篇论文的讨论部分首先根据实验结果提炼出核心要点——2—6月的 ASD 婴儿就与正常婴儿有所区别。随后从较为直观的发育角度和更深层的基因角度对该研究结果展开讨论，给出该现象背后可能的机制解释。

讨论的第二部分更多是对研究展开评价。在回顾了开篇提出的研究问题后，作者比较了本研究与现有研究或理论的异同，有力地增加了论文的深度和广度。同时，作者在与他人研究的关联过程中，巧妙地同步提出了本研究的意义与局限。最后，从 ASD 的发病机制与治疗手段角度，探讨了潜在应用与后续展望。

这篇论文的讨论部分呈现了三角形结构：从具体实验结果，到结果阐释，到意义与展望。从小到大，由点及面，将研究内容与意义进行了极大的拓展。

3. 写作模型

结构要素	说明
总结并解释核心研究结果	总结部分不需要过多重复，精简提炼最核心的研究结果即可，并对该结果给出一些合理的解释与推论。
与现有研究关联比较	上承研究结果，下启研究评价。与既往研究相似可以一定程度上增加本研究的可靠性，相异可凸显研究的创新性。
对相关领域知识的贡献 （本研究的意义和不足、展望）	从客观的角度拓展研究内容与意义，增加论文的深度与广度。

练习2

作者：廖敏如（中国科学院大学2022级硕士生）

论文摘要 [1]

TAO S, CHAVE J, FRISON P, et al. Increasing and widespread vulnerability of intact tropical rainforests to repeated droughts [J]. Proceedings of the National Academy of Sciences of the United States of America, 2022, 119(37): e2116626119.

【研究背景】①Intact tropical rainforests have been exposed to severe droughts in recent decades, which may threaten their integrity, their ability to sequester carbon, and their capacity to provide shelter for biodiversity. ②However, their response to droughts remains uncertain due to limited high-quality, long-term observations covering extensive areas.【研究方法】③Here, we examined how the upper canopy of intact tropical rainforests has responded to drought events globally and during the past 3 decades. ④By developing a long pantropical time series (1992 to 2018) of monthly radar satellite observations,【结果分析】we show that repeated droughts caused a sustained decline in radar signal in 93%, 84%, and 88% of intact tropical rainforests in the Americas, Africa, and Asia, respectively. ⑤Sudden decreases in radar signal were detected around the 1997–1998, 2005, 2010, and 2015 droughts in tropical Americas; 1999–2000, 2004–2005, 2010–2011, and 2015 droughts in tropical Africa; and 1997–1998, 2006, and 2015 droughts in tropical Asia. ⑥Rainforests showed similar low resistance (the ability to maintain predrought condition when drought occurs) to severe droughts across continents, but American rainforests consistently showed the lowest resilience (the ability to return to predrought condition after the drought event). ⑦Moreover, while the resistance of intact tropical rainforests to drought is decreasing, albeit weakly in tropical Africa and Asia, forest resilience has not increased significantly. 【讨论】⑧Our results therefore suggest the capacity of intact rainforests to withstand future droughts is limited. ⑨This has negative implications for climate change mitigation through forest-based climate solutions and the associated pledges made by countries under the Paris Agreement.

论文摘要 [2]

WANG H, YAN S, CIAIS P, et al. Exploring complex water stress-gross primary production relationships: Impact of climatic drivers, main effects, and interactive effects [J]. Global Change Biology, 2022, 28 (13): 4110-4123.

【研究背景】①The dominance of vapor pressure deficit (VPD) and soil water content (SWC) for plant water stress is still under debate. These two variables are strongly coupled and influenced by climatic drivers. ②The impacts of climatic drivers on the relationships between gross primary production (GPP) and water stress from VPD/SWC and the interaction between VPD and SWC are not fully understood. 【研究方法】③Here, applying statistical methods and extreme gradient boosting models-Shapley additive explanations framework to eddy-covariance observations from the global FLUXNET2015 data set, 【结果分析】we found that the VPD-GPP relationship was strongly influenced by climatic interactions and that VPD was more important for plant water stress than SWC across most plant functional types when we removed the effect of main climatic drivers, e.g. air temperature, incoming shortwave radiation and wind speed. ④However, we found no evidence for a significant influence of elevated CO_2 on stress alleviation, possibly because of the short duration of the records (approximately one decade). ⑤Additionally, the interactive effect between VPD and SWC differed from their individual effect. ⑥When SWC was high, the SHAP interaction value of SWC and VPD on GPP was decreased with increasing VPD, but when SWC was low, the trend was the opposite.⑦Additionally, we revealed a threshold effect for VPD stress on GPP loss; above the threshold value, the stress on GPP was flattened off. 【讨论】⑧Our results have important implications for independently identifying VPD and SWC limitations on plant productivity, which is meaningful for capturing the magnitude of ecosystem responses to water stress in dynamic global vegetation models.

论文摘要 [3]

FU Y H, LI X, CHEN S, et al. Soil moisture regulates warming responses of autumn photosynthetic transition dates in subtropical forests [J]. Global Change Biology, 2022, 28(16): 4935-4946.

【研究背景】①Autumn phenology plays a key role in regulating the terrestrial carbon and water balance and their feedbacks to the climate. ②However, the mechanisms underlying autumn phenology are still poorly understood, especially in subtropical forests. 【研究方法】③In this study, we extracted the autumn photosynthetic transition dates (APTD) in subtropical China over the period 2003–2017 based on a global, fine-resolution solar-induced chlorophyll fluorescence (SIF) dataset (GOSIF) using four fitting methods, and then explored the temporal-spatial variations of APTD and its underlying mechanisms using partial correlation analysis and machine learning methods. ④We further predicted the APTD shifts under future climate warming conditions by applying process-based and machine learning-based models. 【结果分析】⑤We found that the APTD was significantly delayed, with an average rate of 7.7 days per decade, in subtropical China during 2003–2017. ⑥Both partial correlation analysis and machine learning methods revealed that soil moisture was the primary driver responsible for the APTD changes in southern subtropical monsoon evergreen forest (SEF) and middle subtropical evergreen forest (MEF), whereas solar radiation controlled the APTD variations in the northern evergreen-broadleaf deciduous mixed forest (NMF). ⑦Combining the effects of temperature, soil moisture and radiation, we found a significantly delayed trend in APTD during the 2030–2100 period, but the trend amplitude (0.8 days per decade) was much weaker than that over 2003–2017. ⑧In addition, we found that machine learning methods outperformed process-based models in projecting APTD.【讨论】⑨Our findings generate from different methods highlight that soil moisture is one of the key players in determining autumn photosynthetic phenological processes in subtropical forests. ⑩To comprehensively understand autumn phenological processes, in-situ manipulative experiments are urgently needed to quantify the contributions of different environmental and physiological factors in regulating plants' response to ongoing climate change.

论文摘要 ［4］

ZHANG Y, FENG X, FU B, et al. Satellite-observed global terrestrial vegetation production in response to water availability ［J］. Remote Sensing, 2021, 13(7): 1-20.

【研究背景】①Water stress is one of the primary environmental factors that limits terrestrial ecosystems' productivity. ②Hense, the way to quantify global vegetation productivity's vulnerability under water stress and reveal its seasonal dynamics in response to drought is of great significance in mitigating and adapting to global changes.【研究方法】③Here, we estimated monthly gross primary productivity (GPP) first based on light-use efficiency (LUE) models for 1982-2015. ④GPP's response time to water availability can be determined by correlating the monthly GPP series with the multiple timescale Standardized Precipitation Evapotranspiration Index (SPEI). ⑤Thereafter, we developed an optimal bivariate probabilistic model to derive the vegetation productivity loss probabilities under different drought scenarios using the copula method.【结果分析】⑥The results showed that LUE models have a good fit and estimate GPP well (R-2 exceeded 0.7). ⑦GPP is expected to decrease in 71.91% of the global land vegetation area because of increases in radiation and temperature and decreases in soil moisture during drought periods. ⑧Largely, we found that vegetation productivity and water availability are correlated positively globally. ⑨The vegetation productivity in arid and semiarid areas depends considerably upon water availability compared to that in humid and semi-humid areas. ⑩Weak drought resistance often characterizes the land cover types that water availability influences more. ⑪In addition, under the scenario of the same level of GPP damage with different drought degrees, as droughts increase in severity, GPP loss probabilities increase as well. ⑫Further, under the same drought severity with different levels of GPP damage, drought's effect on GPP loss probabilities weaken gradually as the GPP damage level increase. ⑬Similar patterns were observed in different seasons.【讨论】⑭Our results showed that arid and semiarid areas have higher conditional probabilities of vegetation productivity losses under different drought scenarios.

论文摘要 [5]

GAMPE D, ZSCHEISCHLER J, REICHSTEIN M, et al. Increasing impact of warm droughts on northern ecosystem productivity over recent decades [J]. Nature Climate Change, 2021, 11(9): 772-779.

【研究背景】①Climate extremes such as droughts and heatwaves have a large impact on terrestrial carbon uptake by reducing gross primary production (GPP). ②While the evidence for increasing frequency and intensity of climate extremes over the last decades is growing, potential systematic adverse shifts in GPP have not been assessed. 【研究方法】③Using observationally-constrained and process-based model data, 【结果分析】we estimate that particularly northern midlatitude ecosystems experienced a +10.6% increase in negative GPP extremes in the period 2000−2016 compared to 1982−1998. ④We attribute this increase predominantly to a greater impact of warm droughts, in particular over northern temperate grasslands (+95.0% corresponding mean increase) and croplands (+84.0%), in and after the peak growing season. 【讨论】⑤These results highlight the growing vulnerability of ecosystem productivity to warm droughts, implying increased adverse impacts of these climate extremes on terrestrial carbon sinks as well as a rising pressure on global food security.

我的专业是生态学，研究方向是生态系统生态学。生态学领域的学术论文摘要部分包含研究背景、研究方法、结果分析和讨论四个部分。首先作者一般会概述现有生态背景，如气候变化、二氧化碳浓度上升等，接着引出这个背景下某个科学问题的研究。紧接着是研究方法，这部分占比通常较少。大部分论文可能更加关注客观结果背后反映的规律，结果分析的占比一般是摘要的重要部分。摘要最后一般是讨论，这一部分占比较小却不可或缺。各部分占比不是绝对的，像文献［3］、［4］中研究方法中的数据和方案较为新颖，占比会有所侧重。因此在写作时，我们可以提炼文章的重点部分和创新点，合理分配每一部分。

文献	研究背景	研究方法	结果分析	讨论
［1］	①、②	③、④前半句	④后半句、⑤、⑥、⑦	⑧、⑨
［2］	①	②、③前半句	④、⑤、⑥、⑦	⑧
［3］	①、②	③、④	⑤、⑥、⑦、⑧	⑨、⑩
［4］	①、②	③、④、⑤	⑥、⑦、⑧、⑨、⑩、⑪、⑫、⑬	⑭
［5］	①、②	③前半句	③后半句、④	⑤

摘要部分的写作模型如下：

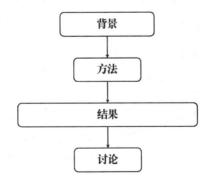

练习3

答案略。

第四讲

练习 1

作者：张宇翔（中国科学院大学 2022 级博士研究生）

这个段落共有 10 句。作者首先在全球疫情大背景下，指明新冠病毒的危害，凸显了本研究的意义和价值。紧接着，向读者说明了疫苗研发中出现的两个问题，其中病毒突变株是疫苗效果不佳的主要原因。针对病毒的高突变特性，介绍了可以有效解决上述问题的一种药物，但是该药物在使用中存在一定的限制，影响了有效性。通过指出当前药物的不足，引出本文开发的新型治疗方法。下面是对段落内部句与句承接关系的分析。

第一句介绍研究背景，即目前的全球疫情。major 和 global 两个形容词体现了其危害较大，从而突出了本文的研究价值。

第二句 pandemics 一词再次出现，和上句形成呼应，并指明这次疫情的元凶是新型冠状病毒，即 coronavirus SARS-CoV-2。另外，该句采用现在完成时，强调了新冠病毒从暴发到现在产生的持续影响。

第三句中，作者将感染与死亡人数呈现出来，说明新冠病毒对人类健康造成的严重危害。该句主语使用 virus，指代上一句中的 coronavirus SARS-CoV-2。

在前三句指出新冠病毒对人类健康的严重危害后，作者转向人类通过开发疫苗来应对危机的举措。其中，第四句中的疫苗（vaccines）、监管机构（regulatory agencies），第五句中的感染（infection）和第一至三句中的病毒（virus）、疫情（pandemic）在同一个语义场，形成了隐性的语义连贯。

第五句句首的 Moreover 起到增补功能，将目前开发存在的两重困难（成本和有效性）连接起来。第五句中的 vaccinations 也和第四句中的 vaccines 形成了很好的照应。

第六句句首的 The situation 指代上句中的疫苗有效性问题。将上一句的具体内容"打包"到有一定抽象意义的 The situation 后，作者指出这个问题的主要原因，即病毒突变株问题，这也是整篇文章要重点解决的问题。

第七句句首代词 This 指代上句病毒突变株的出现。对于病毒易突变的特性，作者在第七句中给出了解决的思路，即要研发和完善治疗方法，通过持续地推陈出新应对各种各样的突变株类型。

第八句介绍了针对病毒突变株的问题，当前使用较为广泛的一种治疗药物。句首的 Therapeutic approaches 和前句的 efficient therapies 形成照应。句中的 only 表明了这种药物还不是理想的治疗方案。

第九句解释了为什么这种药物的治疗效果不好。作者使用 One reason 表明了第八、九句的因果联系。此外，句中的 also 起到增补作用，解释了效果差的另一个原因。

这种药物的治疗效果不尽如人意，需要提供新的方案来。在 Therefore 的引导下，第十句给出了具体解决思路，即在病毒感染细胞前中和病毒。

练习 2

作者：高心洁（中国科学院大学 2020 级硕士研究生）

Li, Y., & Flowerdew, J. (2022). Chinese attitudes to plagiarism: a genre analysis of editorial statements on plagiarism cases (1950s–1960s). *Ethics & Behavior.* https://doi.org/10.1080/10508422.2022.2111307

这篇文章对 20 世纪 50 年代初至 60 年代初在中国期刊上发表的关于剽窃案例的编辑声明进行了综合性的体裁分析和话语分析，总结了此类体裁中的 12 种修辞语步，以及该体裁与两种相关文体（读者举报信和剽窃者道歉声明）之间的互文联系，以此说明中国学术界对剽窃坚决抵制的态度，并在"批评"与"自我批评"的时代背景下对这样的态度做了分析。

① Plagiarism is a discursive practice involving conceptions of creativity, originality, authorship, and transgression. With the increasing globalization of university education and academic research, the issue is an important real-world concern. An influential view with regard to plagiarism is that its conception and attitudes toward it may vary according to cultural traditions. This relativist position has been propounded in the literature concerning Confucian-heritage cultures (CHCs) in particular. It is argued that plagiarism, in the sense of reusing others' words as one's own without proper acknowledgment, is acceptable (or even encouraged) in CHCs, such as China, because imitation and memorization of classics and well-written texts are highly valued traditional literacy practices in these cultures (e.g., Matalene, 1985; Sowden, 2005). Others, however, have argued that plagiarism or claiming ownership of others' text has never been acceptable in CHCs and that repetition being valued as a learning practice in these cultures is a separate issue (e.g., Liu, 2005; Phan Le Ha, 2006). Complementary to this argument, empirical evidence demonstrates that if provided with detailed instruction on source-based writing and given the opportunity of socializing into the rigorous source-use standards expected in the Anglo-American context, learners from CHCs will develop an enhanced awareness for the issue of plagiarism and their writing skills will be honed to enable them to reduce textual transgression (e.g., Gu & Brooks, 2008; Lei & Hu, 2015; Ting, 2012; Wheeler, 2009). Likewise opposing a cultural-conditioning view of plagiarism, we followed a historical, text-based orientation in our own research. In a previous study, we examined the use of Chinese equivalents of "plagiarism" in classical Chinese texts and pointed out that plagiarism has been consistently condemned in China, since the fifth century B.C. (Li & Flowerdew, 2019). In addition, based on textual evidence culled from the 1950s-2010s, we argued that the understanding of the concept of plagiarism in the Chinese context is related to the social-cultural environment of the country (Li & Flowerdew, 2019). **However, further systematic and detailed evidence is needed to support this claim.**

Targeting selected historical periods of time and examining their textual landscapes would be potentially productive for generating such evidence. In the present paper, accordingly, we explore the conceptualization of plagiarism in China in the decade between the early 1950s and the early 1960s, i.e., the period following the founding of the People's Republic of China in 1949 and before the outbreak of the Cultural Revolution in 1966, when the decade-long turmoil largely halted the country's academic publishing. We believe the issue of plagiarism is worth investigating in other periods of time too in classical, modern, and contemporary China. A study of the case of the decade between the early 1950s and the early 1960s, the first decade of new China, is interesting as the insights about the decade can potentially be used as a baseline for comparison with the decades before and after this historical period.

上述段落选自引言部分的前两段。关于剽窃与文化的关系，作者介绍了两种不同的观点，并在中国语境中，表明了自身的立场。"However"一句，指出证实这一立场需要更加系统和充分的证据，对下一段的内容做出"预告"。紧接着，第二段介绍了本研究中证据的收集。因此，这句话起到了很好的过渡作用，可视为一个"指针句"。

② A genre is a typified rhetorical action formulated in a typified social situation to fulfil a particular communicative purpose (Miller, 1994; Swales, 1990). Genres do not exist in isolation but are intertextually linked together in chains or sets. For example, the editorial statements on plagiarism cases, which are the focus of this study, are reactions to a plagiaristic text and may oftentimes follow a reader's disclosure report, and may in turn be followed by an apology from the plagiarizer, as indicated above. A genre has typical content, with its communicative purpose fulfilled through a series of rhetorical stages or move types. The unit of analysis for moves (and their sub-moves or "steps") is a function-based discourse unit, which can be part of a sentence or span across several sentences. These stages or move types can be expressed as labels that capture the dominant communicative goals of the discourse units in an instance of a genre. The moves may be found recurring across the texts of the same genre; some moves may be more frequent or even obligatory, while other moves may be less frequent or optional. A collection of exemplars of the same genre thus tends to display a schematic pattern (Bhatia, 1993; Swales, 1990). A genre is also dynamic in nature (Berkenkotter & Huckin, 1995), which means that its typical content and rhetorical manifestations may shift somewhat with its "chronotope," or time-space (Bakhtin, 1981). In other words, a genre can only be understood well if a researcher aims to understand it within its social context. The time-space in which a genre is located is key to understanding its content, rhetorical structure, and its rhetorical features. Thus, the particular socio-political environment of China in the 1950s-60s will have its imprints on the editorial statements which will be the focus of this study.

To achieve our research goal, in addition to the insights provided by genre analysis as just outlined, we also draw upon Fairclough's (1992) social theory of discourse to shed light on our focal genre in Chinese journals in the 1950s-60s. In Fairclough's (1992) theory, discourse is a three-dimensional conception: discourse as text (analysis of linguistic features), discourse as discursive practice (analysis of rhetorical moves and intertextuality in our study), and discourse as social practice (analysis of the ideological processes in which the discourse operates). From our perspective, the analyses along the first two dimensions echo genre analysis with a critical edge, while the third dimension prompts us to seek explanations of our focal genre in relation to the socio-political environment of China in the historical time in which the instances of the genre were produced.

这两段选自引言中的"理论基础"部分。第一段阐述了体裁分析法对于中国20世纪50年代至60年代的编辑声明研究的理论价值。第二段第一句话可视为一个承上启下的"指针句"。其中"in addition to"回顾总结了上文的内容，紧接着引出本段所要介绍的内容，即Fairclough的社会话语理论对本研究的理论价值。

③ In a preliminary intertextual profile of the focal genre in the Methods section earlier, we already pointed out that an editorial statement is intertextually linked with the other texts in the genre chain of which it is a part: the original author's text, the plagiaristic text, a reader's disclosure report (R), and the plagiarizer's apology (P). Our intertextual analysis of the focal genre in relation to the genres of readers' disclosure reports (R) and plagiarizers' apologies (P) indicate that there are both rhetorical moves shared among them, and rhetorical moves in them that echo each other. Table 4 draws upon our overall analysis of the CPCC1950s-60s to illustrate such intertextual connections.

Table 4 shows that readers' disclosure reports (R) and editorial statements (E) have five rhetorical moves in common with each other, and that when these two genres are considered together with plagiarizers' apologies (P), various moves found in the genre chain echo each other. Such intertextuality among the three genres of E, R, and P highlights the fact that the editorial statements focused on in the present study are part of a larger picture. The discourse of criticism and self-criticism evident in the genre chain at the same time contributed toward a much broader intertextuality with the discourse of criticism and self-criticism present in society at large in China in the 1950s-60s, as promoted by Mao and the Chinese Communist Party, and as referred to in our earlier section on the socio-historical context.

这两段选自"结果和讨论"部分。第一段介绍了研究结果中体现出读者举报信和剽窃者道歉声明这两种文体有共用的语步和相互呼应的语步。结尾句聚焦至具体的结果,指出表格4通过对语料库中20世纪50至60年代的数据分析证明了这种文体之间的联系,为下一段中对表格4的详细描述做出预告,使上下文衔接更为自然,可视为一个"指针句"。

练习3

第一段的画线句和前一句的连接不够紧密:人们在汤洒了之后的懊恼和自我提醒通常是短暂的,称不上是"深思"(consideration)或"探索"(exploration),此处可以借用英谚"It is no use crying over the split milk"的相关表达,将此句改为:Instead of crying over the spilt soup, one may turn to deep explorations of the spillage phenomenon.

第二段的画线句和前一段的连接不够紧密:由于第一段没有任何地方提到coffee,本句开头的The question "why does coffee spill"中的coffee显得非常突兀。此外,画线的前后两句连接也不够紧密,可以将前后两句的信息合并。本划线句可修改为:Previous studies on liquid spillage, casting the most attention on coffee spillage, recognized liquid resonance and hand postures as two critical factors.

第五讲

练习1

(1) It is also generally believed a trust crisis exists in today's society, and thus studying people's trust tendency is of great importance.

(2) Wang et al. (2005) summarized six factors influencing trust among people, namely, social similarity, degree of knowing other people, personal perspective on his/her own personality, social status, social culture background and law.

(3) This finding uncovered the importance of the "lead-in process", in which the subjects participate in or are led into the experiments.

(4) Two additional situations, similar to two of the seventeen situations, were added in the questionnaire to check if the questionnaire had been finished earnestly.

(5) X^2 test shows that gender and college students' trust tendency showed obvious relativity ($K^2=3.922$, $P>0.95$), but the relevance between major and trust propensity and personality and trust tendency was not so distinct ($K^2=0.920$, $P<0.75$; $K^2=0.268$, $P<0.5$).

练习 2

(1) Studies on slime mold focus on its area extension on plain plates, but investigation in their extension on angled plates remained blank.

(2) Though many excellent conclusions have been drawn by previous studies, some unsolved problems left.

(3) Our analyses revealed that the slime mold has the "gravitropic responses", yet we have no solid evidence to show the slime mold' growth is highly affected by magnetic environment.

(4) One weakness in the experiment is that the controlled conditions are not strict enough. Another is that the sample size is not big enough.

(5) Though the growing speed was influenced, little impact was found in terms of the direction the slime mold chose.

练习 3

(1) Still, the study has a few limitations and challenges that the future research should consider.

(2) Although the result has shown the superiority of M/M/c queuing form based on the statistic collected from UCAS, we fail to give the proof under common conditions.

(3) Although our experimental results did not meet the expecta-

tions, they reveal what should be paid attention to in material selection, and provide guidance for the subsequent related experiments.

(4) Notably, despite that our results are less than satisfactory compared with our prediction, we are the first to carry out research on the relationship between music preferences and the mastering of instruments within our range of knowledge.

(5) Although there are some significant discoveries shown this study, there are still several limitations.

句（2）和句（5）将研究的不足放到了主句中，使得研究的不足凸显了出来。尤其是句（2），使用了 We 做主语，fail 做谓语动词，使得研究的不足更加凸显。句（3）和句（4）将研究的不足放到了从句中，弱化了研究的不足，凸显了其优点。

第六讲

练习 1.1

（1）这句话表意很不精确。most respondents 的含义很模糊，最好能给出百分比。

（2）这句话里的 customization 表意不清晰，作者想表达的应该是"订阅"而不是"订制"；此外 missed points 的表意也不清晰，作者想表达的可能是"课堂上漏听的知识点"。此句可改为：Nine percent of our respondents subscribed online courses to learn the knowledge points that they missed or are not taught in class.

练习 1.2

（1）可重写为：This study was to investigate how university students was affected by iPads.

（2）可重写为：Specifically, for one thing, notetaking apps on iPad are good platforms where information can be well-kept and easy to move and sort through.

（3）可重写为：Notability provides limitless spaces for drafting and recording fleeting inspirations, while Goodnotes with more than 20 styles can satisfy individual needs for typography and its diverse marking colors facilitate note-highlighting.

练习 1.3

（1）可修改为：The results show that respondents mainly benefited from note-taking apps and video apps that facilitate their course learning.

（2）可修改为：We also concluded through our survey that writing on the screen with Apple Pencil is convenient, and so it is with tailoring knowledge points from PDF files.

（3）可修改为：Although a few respondents reported they are more likely to be distracted by entertainment apps due to their easy access, a greater number of respondents reported that iPad helps them engage more and sustain longer concentration in class.

（4）可修改为：If we adopt practical measures to reduce distraction (e.g., using time management apps), the benefits of using iPad for study will be maximized.

练习 2

作者：董国丹（中国科学院大学工程科学学院 2021 级硕士生）

1

修改前	修改后
To evaluate the predictive capability of the non-uniformly loaded actuator disk (AD) models in simulating wakes of different windturbine designs of utility-scale, large-eddy simulations (LESs) of the 2.5 MW EOLOS wind turbine, the 5 MW NREL wind turbine, and a variant of the 5 MW NREL wind turbine are carried out.	To evaluate the predictive capability of the actuator disk (AD) models in simulating wakes of different wind turbine designs, we *compare* the results of the AD simulation with those of the actuator surface (AS) simulation for the EOLOS, NREL and *a variant of the NREL (i.e., NREL-V) wind turbine designs*.

分析：(1) EOLOS 和 NREL 风机是行业众所周知的实用大尺度风力发电机，这些风机的功率也是行业众所周知的，因此去掉了这部分赘余，使句子更简洁；(2) 在下文我们说明了 AD 的力系数分布是如何得到的，因此删掉了 non-uniformly loaded 这一赘余部分；(3) 在我们新设计的风机 a variant of the NREL 后加上了 (i.e., NREL-V)，这样下文可以直接使用 NREL-V 来代指新设计的风力机；(4) 将 are carried out 改为 compare，用主动形式表达，使句子更有活力。

2

修改前	修改后
Since countries all over the world commit to be carbon neural in the next few decades, more and more research efforts to reduce the levelized cost of wind energy is called because wind energy is renewable and sustainable.	*The commitment* of countries to become carbon neural in the next few decades *calls* for *increasing* research efforts to reduce the levelized cost of wind energy because of its *renewability and sustainability*.

分析：(1) 将 commit 改为 commitment，renewable 和 sustainable 改为 renewability 和 sustainability，通过将动词和形容词名词化，使句子更简洁；(2) 将 more and more 改为 increasing，使句子更简洁；(3) 将 countries all over the word 改为 countries，使句子更简洁；(4) 将 is called 改为 calls，主动语态的使用使句子更有活力。

3

修改前	修改后
The wake dynamics is of great importance. In order to understand this, many researchers studied the wake dynamics by investigating the interactions between wakes.	*Continuous research effort has been made* to understand the *mechanism* of the wake dynamics.

分析：(1) 将 In order to understand 改为 to understand，使句子更简洁；(2) 第一句话有些突兀，因此删掉，用 continuous research effort 来开头；（3）将 investigating the interactions between wakes 用一个词 mechanism 取代，在不改变句意的情况下，更简洁易读；（4）将 studied 改为 has been made 表示目前还在进行尾迹机理的研究，使句子表意更准确。

4

修改前	修改后
Instead of using this, wind turbines are often modelled to reduce the computational cost. Specifically, the actuator disk (AD) model that represents the turbine blades as a disk, the actuator line (AL) model that represents the turbine blades as three lies, and the actuator surface (AS) model that represents the turbine blades as three surfaces are commonly used in the wind turbine models.	*Instead*, wind turbines are often *parametrized* with actuator type models to reduce the computational cost, including the actuator disk (AD) model, the actuator line (AL) model and the actuator surface (AS) model.

分析：（1）将 Instead of using this, 改为 Instead, 在不改变句意的情况下使用更简洁的短语；（2）第二个句子去掉多余的 that represents the turbine blades as a disk, that represents the turbine blades as three lies 和 that represents the turbine blades as three surfaces are commonly used in the wind turbine models, 使句子更简洁；（3）加上 actuator type models 总领后面的 AD, AL 和 AS, 表意更清晰；（4）AD, AL 是风机叶片参数化模型，将 modelled 改为 parametrized, 在句意表达上更为准确。

5

修改前	修改后
We test AD models with non-uniformly distributed axial forces and tangential forces, which are obtained from the AS simulations, with the one with and without rotational effect denoted as AD-R and AD-NR models, respectively.	*Two types of* AD models *(with and without the rotational effect, which are denoted as the AD-R and the AD-NR models, respectively) are considered.*

分析：（1）本句介绍了我们研究的两种 AD 模型，加了没有必要的修饰 with non-uniformly distributed axial forces and tangential forces 和 which are obtained from the AS simulations 后，句子读起来很费劲，故删掉；（2）将 with the one with and without rotational effect denoted as AD-R and AD-NR models 这部分内容放在 two types of AD models 后面的括号里，使句子主次分明，表意清晰；（3）在 AD models 前面加上 two types 的限定，与括号里面的两种 AD 模型形成呼应；（4）将 test 改为 are considered，使用被动，使表达更显客观。

第七讲

练习 1

图表所列七种情形都属于剽窃，无论我们直接引用他人语言/观点，还是间接转述他人观点、整合不同文献中的观点，都应该明示出处，规范征引。

练习 2

示例文献：WETTE R. Evaluating student learning in a university-level EAP unit on writing using sources [J]. Journal of Second Language Writing, 2010, 19 (3): 158–177.

该文献在 Research Gate 网站显示被引 96 次。现列举三处：

(1) LAI M W C. Uncovering the complexities in writing from sources from an activity theory perspective: A cross-case analysis of Chinese International graduate students in education [D]. Toronto: University of Toronto, 2022.

"Empirical evidence has shown that these interventions boosted student writers' abilities to write more effectively (e.g., Hendricks & Quinn, 2000; Wette, 2010; Zhang, 2013)."

(2)CHEN W H, WANG J J. Understanding source use by undergraduate post-novice EFL writers for the sustainability development of academic literacy: Abilities, challenges, and strategies [J]. Sustainability, 2022, 14, 2108.

"For example, through detailed textual analysis of essays written before and after instruction, Wette [52] uncovered a significant increase in the incidence of accurate summaries and a decrease in the proportion of copying (i.e., plagiarism), although students' efforts to use sources were sometimes not successful."

(3)SUN X Y, HU G W. What do academics know and do about plagiarism? An interview study with Chinese university teachers of English [J]. Ethics & Behavior, 2020, 30 (6): 459-479.

"Wette's (2010) action research at a university in New Zealand confirmed that an instructional intervention was effective in improving a group of ESL students' awareness, knowledge, and skills concerning source-based writing."

上述三处引用均汇报了 Wette (2010) 年研究论文的主要发现，但在详略程度和侧重点上有所差异。第一篇文章的概述最为简略（和其他两篇文献放在群引中，突出结果的共性）；第二篇和第三篇引述较为详尽。其中，第二篇突出学生在教学干预之后转述和概括方面技能的提升；第三篇则侧重学生经过教学干预在意识、知识、技能多方面的提升。

练习 3

作者：刘静怡（中国科学院大学 2019 级博士研究生）

ZHANG X, ZHANG H, GU J, et al. Engineered extracellular vesicles for cancer therapy [J]. Advanced Material. 2021, 33, 2005709. https://doi.org/10.1002/adma.202005709

这篇综述介绍了工程化的胞外囊泡在癌症治疗中的应用，以下两个段落介绍了细胞外囊泡的来源和成分。后文是我对作者如何有效使用引用，凸显自身声音的一些分析。

Although the mechanisms responsible for specific cargo sorting in EVs are still unclear, previous studies have proposed several possibilities. For example, protein molecules are sorted into MVBs in a ubiquitin-dependent manner with the help of endosomal sorting complex required for transport. In addition, tetraspanin-enriched microdomains also contribute to the sorting of proteins into EVs[18]. For specific loading of RNAs, mainly microRNAs (miRNAs), into EVs, several key factors such as heterogeneous nuclear ribonucleoprotein A2B1 (hnRNPA2B1),[19] adenylation and urylation at the 3′ end of miRNAs,[20] argonaute 2 (Ago2),[21] and ubiquitinated form of human antigen R (HuR)[22] have been reported to be critically involved. Clancy et al. suggest that the interaction between ADP-ribosylation factor 6 (ARF6)-GTP and Exportin-5 promotes pre-miRNA cargo sorting into tumor MVs.[23] Intriguingly, the specific cargos in EVs could reflect the pathophysiological status of their parental cells, which makes them useful biomarkers for monitoring disease progression.[5] The lipid bilayer membrane structure of EVs not only protects internal proteins and nucleic acids from degradation, but also maintains the inherent targeting abilities from their parental cells, which endows them the potential to serve as an effective carrier for delivering cargos into recipient cells. Moreover, the specific lipidomic and proteomic profiles of EVs may help them escape from endosomal traps and allow for a direct cytosolic delivery of therapeutic cargos.[9,17] These natural and unique properties make EVs ideal NVs for drug delivery.

However, there are some hurdles when translating EVs from bench to bedside. The low isolation yield and complicated purification protocols make massive production of EVs a challenging task. Thus, it is urgently needed to develop standard, scalable, and cost-effective approaches for EV production. In addition, due to the considerable heterogeneity of isolated EVs and their complex composition and structure, it is difficult to characterize EVs as synthetic nanoparticles (NPs) that are currently used in the clinic (e.g., liposomes). Moreover, tedious cargo loading procedures, relatively low delivery efficiency, and unsatisfactory targeting ability also hinder the therapeutic applications of EVs. If these main problems are properly solved, the applicability of EVs as therapeutic NVs will be greatly advanced.

　　首句作者指出，虽然现在关于细胞外囊泡包含的组分的机制尚未完全清楚，但有很多研究者对它的可能性进行了分析。之后列举的他人工作是对现有发现和研究的举例说明。紧接着，作者指出，细胞外囊泡除了丰富的内容物，还有着稳定的磷脂双分子层膜结构，可以保护内容物，防止其外泄。此外，还可以提供靶向的功能，进一步强调了细胞外囊泡的组成优势。作者并没有过多地陈述他人的工作是如何详细地研究以及他们所研究的内容具体是什么，而是通过他人的研究来佐证自己的观点——细胞外囊泡有着丰富的内容物，以及稳定的膜结构，从生物组成来说，可以作为良好的药物递送载体。

　　下一段作者使用 However 进行转折：在细胞外囊泡具有天然优势的基础上，它实现临床应用的阻碍是什么，为什么大家对它有诸多的研究，它还有什么需要进一步工程化的必要。这也是作者再一次强调了自己综述的主题，由天然优势过渡到它的不足，而引出后续想要说明的工程化。

　　这部分的内容起到了承上启下的作用，从对细胞外囊泡的介绍过渡到对其进行工程化，以及它在癌症治疗中的具体应用。虽然引用了许多他人的工作来陈述细胞外囊泡生物组成的可能性，但是并不是简单的铺陈，而是通过他人的工作来强调细胞外囊泡的组成优势，着重强调了它在癌症治疗中应用的可能性。通过这样的方式，作者也避免了自己的观点被大量引用淹没的情况出现。

第八讲

练习 1

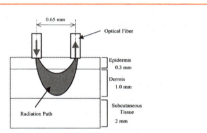

FIG. 1. Concept of blood glucose measurement; schematic diagram of the cross-section of skin tissue at the forearm and the radiation path.

Type: Figure (Diagram)

Source: Author's own research data

Description: As shown in Fig.1, one set of optical fibers is attached to the skin surface vertically; the skin surface is illuminated by the measuring radiation through the source optical fiber and the scattered radiation is collected by the detector optical fiber.

Table 4
Comparison of the pre- and post-test source-use appropriateness.

	Pre-test		Post-test		t (29)	P-Value
	M	SD	M	SD		
Attribution to source authors	3.03	1.10	3.60	0.42	−2.50*	.018
Representation of source ideas	2.94	0.81	3.38	0.56	−2.90**	.007
Transformation of source language	1.98	1.03	2.76	0.88	−3.54**	.001
Overall appropriateness	7.95	1.80	9.74	1.08	−4.42**	.000

$^*p < .05$ $^{**}p < .01$.

Type: Table

Source: Author's own research data

Description: Student pre-test writing samples showed a test mean of 3.03 (out of 4) for attribution of authorship, a test mean of 2.94 (out of 4) for representation of source ideas and a test mean of 3.03 (out of 4) for transformation of source language (see Table 4).

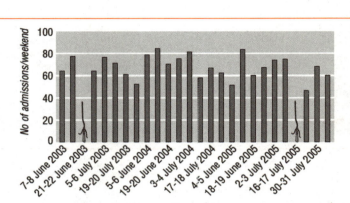

Children attending emergency department with musculoskeletal injuries on summer weekends 2003-5

Type: Figure (Bar Chart)
Source: Official statistics (www.metoffice.gov.uk)
Description: The figure shows the weekend attendance to our emergency department in June and July between 2003 and 2005.

练习2

The figure shows the changing trend of the number of international students enrolled in China from 2004 to 2020. As seen from the line graph, the number of international students coming to China was only about 50,000 in 2004, and then rose steadily in the following five years. Since 2009, the number of international students coming to China has been rising rapidly. In 2019, the number of students studying in China reached more than 170,000, an increase of nearly 100,000 or more than two times compared to 2009.

The rapid growth since 2009 may be attributed to the following three reasons. First, the 2008 Beijing Olympic Games demonstrated China's good national image and enhanced its international influence, which made overseas students have more confidence in China's education; Second, with the establishment of Confucius Institutes overseas, Chinese culture has become more and more popular among overseas young people; Third, with the promotion of "the belt and road initiative", the international cooperation between China and the countries along its route is deepening, and the good employment prospect attracts students from the countries along the "the belt and road initiative" to choose to study in China.

The outbreak of the Covid-19 epidemic at the end of 2019 had a significant impact on overseas students coming to study in China, and the number of students coming to study in China in 2020 was about half of that in 2019. With the normalization of the epidemic and the recovery of international contacts, it can be predicted that the number of international students coming to China will slowly rebound in the next few years.

第九讲

练习

作者：王楚瑜（中国科学院大学 2020 级硕士研究生）

我所在的领域是材料与化工专业，利用老师介绍的写作工具，我修改了一篇自己撰写的题为"Perovskite micro-nano cage $SrTiO_3$: Formation mechanism, vacancy analysis, and exciton dynamics"论文的引言部分。具体过程如下。

第一步：用英文撰写初稿。

①Perovskite oxides are generally studied for their applications in electronics, sensors, catalysts, and energy storage et.al. ②Recent years have witnessed great efforts in the field of high-performance photoelectric materials based on perovskite crystals. ③Strontium titanate ($SrTiO_3$, STO) is a typical perovskite crystal with good electronic properties and high photocatalytic activity ④The single-crystal $SrTiO_3$ with different morphologies and crystal facets presents varied photoelectric properties, and its formation mechanism and structural characteristics become the focus of research. ⑤The different crystal facets of $SrTiO_3$ exhibit different band structures and band edge positions, thus showing different redox characteristics. ⑥T. Takata and et al.[2] demonstrated the relationship between the crystal structure and photon utilization efficiency of $SrTiO_3$ based on hydrogen production through photolysis of water. ⑦They used a modified aluminium-doped $SrTiO_3$ ($SrTiO_3$: Al) photocatalyst, and the external quantum efficiency of the total cracking of water was as high as 96% when (001) and (110) facets were exposed. ⑧Consequently, the optoelectronic properties are very sensitive to the change of the crystal plane, and the crystal facet regulation needs to be paid more attention in the study of the optoelectronic properties of materials.

⑨In order to expose more crystal facets, much attention has been paid to the introduction of crystal facets modifiers. ⑩In our previous research work[6], single-crystalline $SrTiO_3$ particles with different crystal facets were successfully synthesized by adding different acids and alcohols to reactant precursor, which adjusted the process of reactive crystallization $SrTiO_3$. ⑪Simultaneously, Hui and Dong et al. have synthesized shape-controlled $SrTiO_3$ crystals using a series of alcohols varying pKa values or concentrations as facets surfactants. ⑫These surfactants influence the relative surface energy and growth rate of crystal facets, as a result of the different surface absorption energy with Sr and Ti rich crystal facets. ⑬However, optoelectronic properties of crystals are not only affected by the size and type of crystal facets but also affected by grain quality, atomic arrangement, lattice distortion, and defects distribution. ⑭Therefore, it is crucial to further analyze other influencing factors in the growth process mechanism of strontium titanate crystal. ⑮ What's more, the exciton self-trapping effect in perovskite structure is closely related to the lifetime of photogenerated carries, but it's rarely exploited in SrTiO$_3$.

第二步：利用软件 Grammarly 对全文的拼写、标点和语法进行修改。

（1）第⑥句的 "T. Takata and et al." 中，句中的 "and" 是多余的，这是在写作中因粗心犯的错误。"et al." 是拉丁文中 "et alia" 的缩写，其含义为 "and others"，因此句中 "and" 应删去。

（2）第⑦句的 "a modified aluminium-doped SrTiO$_3$ (SrTiO$_3$: Al) photocatalyst" 中，"aluminium" 显示拼写错误，建议修改为 "aluminum"。查阅资料发现，两种拼写都是可以的：北美国家较常写成 "aluminum"；其他国家则写成 "aluminium"；国际纯粹与应用物理学联合会（International Union of Pure and Applied Chemistry）更新的元素周期表也写为 "aluminium"。我投稿的期刊是《化学通讯》（*Chemical Communications*），为英国期刊，故不作修改。

（3）第⑧句 "needs to be paid more attention in the study" 中，pay attention 多与介词 to 连用，句中使用被动语态 "……需要被重视"，忽略了介词 to，而后的 in 是指 "在……研究中" 的介词。因此句中的 "in" 前加上 "to"。

（4）第⑩句 "adding different acids and alcohols to reactant precursor" 中，"reactant precursor" 提示了两种修改形式。第一种是

在前面加上"the",特指该反应前驱体;第二种是将"precursor"改为复数形式,泛指化学反应中的前驱体。结合语义,本句特指在我们前期的研究工作,因此采用第一种修改方法。

(5) 第⑪句"a series of alcohols varying pKa values or concentrations"中,"varying pKa values or concentrations"修饰"alcohols",应在"varying"一词前添加 with,做后置定语。

(6) 第⑫句"the different surface absorption energy with Sr and Ti rich crystal facets"中,"Ti rich"想要表达的意思为"富含钛的",而仅仅两个单词放在一起作为形容词的用法不当,应在词中加上连字符,连接成一个概念,构建形容词。而语义上我想表达的是"富含锶的和富含钛的",二者用"and"连接,因此"Sr"后也该改为"Sr-rich",才能更精确地表达语义。

第三步:利用 Linggle,Skell 和 Thesaurus 等网站润色。

第②句中"Recent years have witnessed great efforts …",句中主语为"recent years",但本句的目的是想突出在该领域上已经取得了的进展,因此认为应将"great efforts"作为主语。通过在 SKELL 网站中查找"great efforts"的使用实例,参考以"great efforts"为主语的例子"Greater efforts are required to encourage greater use of mobile technology",将第二句改写为"Great efforts have been undertaken in the field … in recent years."

接着对第⑥句(内容为引用前人的研究内容)进行改写。第⑥句中"crystal structure""photon utilization efficiency""hydrogen production""photolysis of water"都为专业词语，因此得保留。因此，本句主要对"relationship"增加修饰，Linggle 和 SKELL 中都提供了一些高频搭配的形容词，如"working/close/personal/good/new/special"，以及"close/romantic/sexual/intimate/…"。结合语义，选择"close"修饰"relationship"，整个词语表达为"钛酸锶晶体结构与光子利用效率之间的密切关系"，因此改为："demonstrated the close relationship between …"。

第四步：利用 Academic Phrasebank 网站改写部分语句。

在该段落的结尾处，是承上启下引出本文的研究内容，因此需要指出前人的研究空白。第⑮句的问题是对研究空白的描写太少，且"but it's rarely exploited in SrTiO₃"表达的意思不够清晰。

参考在 Academic Phrasebank 网站上找到"突出以往研究的不足"的例句，如"Researchers have not treated X in much detail""Previous studies of X have not dealt with …"，因此可将其改写为："However, researchers have not treated the self-trapping exciton effect of SrTiO$_3$ in much detail."，清楚指出在该领域的研究空白，更好地引出本文的研究内容。

修改后的引言如下：

①Perovskite oxides are generally studied for their applications in electronics, sensors, catalysts, and energy storage et.al. ②Great efforts have been undertaken in the field of high-performance photoelectric materials based on perovskite crystals in recent years. ③Strontium titanate (SrTiO$_3$, STO) is a typical perovskite crystal with good electronic properties and high photocatalytic activity. ④The single-crystal SrTiO$_3$ with different morphologies and crystal facets presents varied photoelectric properties, and its formation mechanism and structural characteristics become the focus of research. ⑤The different crystal facets of SrTiO$_3$ exhibit different band structures and band edge positions, thus showing different redox characteristics[4-5]. ⑥T. Takata et al.[2] demonstrated the close relationship between the crystal structure and photon utilization efficiency of SrTiO$_3$ based on hydrogen production through photolysis of water. ⑦They used a modified aluminium-doped SrTiO$_3$ (SrTiO$_3$: Al) photocatalyst, and the external quantum efficiency of the total cracking of water was as high as 96% when (001) and (110) facets were exposed. ⑧Consequently, the optoelectronic properties are very sensitive to the change of the crystal plane, and the crystal facet regulation needs to be paid more attention to in the study of the optoelectronic properties of materials.

⑨In order to expose more crystal facets, much attention has been paid to the introduction of crystal facets modifiers. ⑩In our previous research work[6], single-crystalline SrTiO$_3$ particles with different crystal facets were successfully synthesized by adding different acids and alcohols to the reactant precursor, which adjusted the process of reactive crystallization SrTiO$_3$. ⑪Simultaneously, Hui and Dong et al. have synthesized shape-controlled SrTiO$_3$ crystals using a series of alcohols with varying pKa values or concentrations as facets surfactants. ⑫These surfactants influence the relative surface energy and growth rate of crystal facets, as a result of the different surface absorption energy with Sr-rich and Ti-rich crystal facets. ⑬However, optoelectronic properties of crystals are not only affected by the size and type of crystal facets but also affected by grain quality, atomic arrangement, lattice distortion, and defects distribution. ⑭Therefore, it is crucial to further analyze other influencing factors in the growth process mechanism of strontium titanate crystal. ⑮ What's more, the exciton self-trapping effect in perovskite structure is closely related to the lifetime of photogenerated carries[9, 10]. However, researchers have not treated the self-trapping exciton effect of SrTiO$_3$ in much detail.

学术写作资源

1. 学术写作专著

（1）学生自学使用

BARROS L O. The only academic phrasebank you'll ever never need: 600 examples of acdemic language [M]. CreateSpace Independent Publishing Platform, 2016.

BELCHER W L. Writing your journal article in twelve weeks [M]. Second edition. Chicago: Chicago University Press, 2019.

CARGILL M, OCONNOR P. Writing scientific research articles: Strategies and steps [M]. Second edition. New Jersey: Wiley-Blackwell, 2013.

GASTEL B, DAY R A. How to write and publish a scientific paper [M]. Ninth edition. Santa Barbara: Greenwood, 2022.

HOWE S, HENRIKSSON K. Phrasebook for writing papers and research in English [M]. Fourth edition. Cambridge: The Whole World Company Press, 2007.

SARAMAKI J. How to write a scientific paper: An academic self-help guide for PhD students [M]. Independently published, 2018.

SCHIMEL J. Writing science: How to write papers that get cited and proposals that get funded [M]. New York: Oxford University Press, 2011.

SILVIA P. How to write a lot: A practical guide to productive academic writing [M]. Second edition. Washington, DC: American Psychological Association, 2019.

SWORD H. Air & Light & Time & Space: How successful academics write [M]. Massachusetts: Harvard University Press, 2017.

TURABIAN K L. A manual for writers of research papers, theses, and dissertations: Chicago style for students and researchers [M]. Nineth edition. Chicago: University of Chicago Press, 2018.

刘军强. 写作是门手艺 [M]. 南宁：广西师范大学出版社，2020.

（2）教师教学参考

ALEXANDER O, ARGENT S, SPENCER J. EAP essentials: A teacher's guide to principles and practice [M]. Second edition. Reading: Garnet education, 2019.

ALLEY M. The craft of scientific writing [M]. Fourth edition. New York: Springer, 2018.

BERGER R E. A scientific approach to writing for engineers and scientists [M]. New Jersey: IEEE press, 2014.

DAY R A, SAKADUSKI N. Scientific English: A guide for scientists and other professionals [M]. Third edition. Santa Barbara: Greenwood, 2011.

FRODESEN J, WALD M. Exploring options in academic writing: Effective vocabulary and grammar use [M]. Ann Arbor: University of Michigan Press, 2016.

GLASMAN-DEAL H. Science research writing for native and non-native speakers of English [M]. Second edition. New Jersey: World Scientific, 2020.

GOPEN G D. The sense of structure: Writing from the reader's perspective [M]. London: Pearson Education Inc, 2004.

GOPEN G D. Expectations: Teaching writing from the reader's perspective [M]. London: Pearson Education Inc, 2004.

HART S. English exposed: Common mistakes by Chinese speakers [M]. Hongkong: Hong Kong University Press, 2017.

HYLAND K. Teaching and researching writing [M]. Third edition. New York: Routledge, 2015.

HYLAND K. English for academic purposes: An advanced resource book [M]. New York: Routledge, 2006.

HYLAND K, SHAW P. The Routledge handbook of English for academic purposes [G]. Abington/New York: Routledge, 2016.

HYLAND K. Metadiscourse: Exploring interaction in writing [M]. London: Continuum, 2005.

ZWIER L J. Building academic vocabulary [G]. Michigan: University of Michigan Press, 2002.

LEBRUN J-L. Scientific writing: A reader and writer's guide [M]. Singapore: World Scientific Writing, 2007.

MOTT-SMITH J A, TOMAS Z, KOSTKA I. Teaching effective source use: Classroom approaches that work [M]. Ann Arbor: University of Michigan Press, 2017.

PECORARI D. Teaching to avoid plagiarism: How to promote good source use [M]. Berkshire: Open University Press, 2013.

SWALES J M. Genre analysis: English in academic and research settings [M]. New York: Cambridge University Press, 1990.

SWALES J M. Research genres: Explorations and applications [M]. New York: Cambridge University Press, 2004.

SWORD H. Stylish academic writing [M]. Cambridge, Massachusetts: Harvard University Press, 2012.

WESTON A. A rulebook for arguments [M]. Fifth edition. Indianapolis: Hackett Publishing Company, 2017.

WETTE R. Writing using sources for academic purposes: Theory, research and practice [M]. New York: Routledge, 2021.

WITHROW J, BROOKS G, CUMMINGS M C. Inspired to write: Readings and tasks to develop writing [G]. New York: Cambridge University Press, 2004.

2. 学术英语教材

(1) 牛津学术英语教材系列(共5个等级)

DE CHAZAL E, HUGHES J. Oxford EAP: A course in English for acdemic purposes elementary/A2［G］. Oxford: Oxford University Press, 2015.

DUMMETT P, HIRD J. Oxford EAP: A course in English for acdemic purposes pre-intermediate/B1［G］. Oxford: Oxford University Press, 2015.

DE CHAZAL E, ROGERS L. Oxford EAP：A course in English for acdemic purposes intermediate/B1+［G］. Oxford: Oxford University Press, 2013.

DE CHAZAL E, MCCARTER S. Oxford EAP: A course in English for acdemic purposes upper-intermediate/B2［G］. Oxford: Oxford University Press, 2012.

DE CHAZAL E, MOORE J. Oxford EAP: A course in English for acdemic purposes advanced/C1［G］. Oxford: Oxford University Press, 2013.

(2) 剑桥学术英语教材系列(共3个等级)

THAINE C, MCCARTHY M. Cambridge academic english B1+ intermediate student's book: An integrated skills course for EAP［G］. Cambridge: Cambridge University Press, 2012.

HEWINGS M, MCCARTHY M. Cambridge academic english B2

upper intermediate student's book: An integrated skills course for EAP［G］. Cambridge: Cambridge University Press, 2012.

HEWINGS M, THAINE C, MCCARTHY M. Cambridge academic english C1 advanced student's book: An integrated skills course for EAP［G］. Cambridge: Cambridge University Press, 2012.

（3）Adrian Wallwork 学术英语系列

WALLWORK A. User guides, manuals, and technical writing: A guide to professional English［M］. New York: Springer, 2014.

WALLWORK A. English for academic research: Grammar, usage and style［M］Second edition. New York: Springer, 2023.

WALLWORK A. English for academic correspondence［M］Second edition. Cham: Springer International Publishing, 2016.

WALLWORK A. English for academic research: Writing exercises［M］. Second edition. New York: Springer, 2024.

WALLWORK A. English for academic research: Vocabulary exercises［M］. Second edition. New York: Springer, 2024.

WALLWORK A. English for academic research: Grammar exercises［M］Second edition. New York: Springer, 2024.

WALLWORK A. English for writing research papers［M］. Second edition. Cham: Springer International Publishing, 2016.

WALLWORK A. English for academic research: A guide for teachers［M］. Cham: Springer International Publishing, 2016.

WALLWORK A. Top 50 grammar mistakes: How to avoid them

(Easy English!)［M］. Cham: Springer International Publishing, 2018.

WALLWORK A. Top 50 vocabulary mistakes: How to avoid them (Easy English!)［M］. Cham: Springer International Publishing, 2018.

WALLWORK A. English for academic CVs, resumes, and online profiles［M］. Cham: Springer International Publishing, 2019.

WALLWORK A, SOUTHERN A. 100 tips to avoid mistakes in academic writing and presenting［M］. Cham: Springer International Publishing, 2020.

（4）其他教材

ARGENT S, ALEXANDER O. Access EAP: Foundations (Course book)［M］. Reading: Garnet education, 2010.

SWALES J M, FEAK C B. Academic Writing for graduate students: Essential tasks and skills［M］. Third Edition. Ann Arbor: The University of Michigan Press, 2012.

3. 高校写作中心

（1）普渡大学在线写作实验室（https://owl.purdue.edu）

大学写作中心的典范，学术写作的资源宝库。

（2）北卡罗莱纳大学写作中心（https://writingcenter.unc.edu/）

该网站导航栏中 Tips and Tools 栏目里有很多独立的资源栏，读者可有针对性地学习，资源按 A-Z 排序。另外，English Language 栏目下设的 Resources 专栏资源丰富。

（3）德州 A&M 大学写作中心（https://writingcenter.tamu.edu/）

该网站导航栏中的 Writing and Speaking Guides 专栏提供了众多独立的资源栏，读者可有针对性地学习，资源按 A-Z 排序。

4. 写作在线课程

（1）Coursera (https://www.coursera.org)

Grammar and Punctuation (University of California, Irvine)

Getting Started with Essay Writing (University of California, Irvine)

Advanced Writing (University of California, Irvine)

Introduction to Research for Essay Writing (University of California, Irvine)

Project: Writing a Research Paper (University of California, Irvine)

（2）Future Learn (https://www.futurelearn.com/courses)

A Beginner's Guide to Writing in English for University Study (University of Reading)

An Intermediate Guide to Writing in English for University Study (University of Reading)

（3）MIT OpenCourseWare (https://ocw.mit.edu)

Advanced workshop in writing for science and engineering (Instructor: Jane Dunphy)

（4）中国大学慕课（https://www.icourse163.org）

学术英语写作（山东大学）

5. 其他

https://www.eapfoundation.com/（专门面向 EAP 学生和教师的网站）

https://www.eapteachingresources.com/（专门面向 EAP 教师的教学资源网站）

后　记

后 记

在北外读书的时候，约是十年前，我得到了去加州大学伯克利分校语言学系访学的机会。我往随身行李箱里塞了一本《认知语言学十讲》，在飞机上读了起来。那本书的内容很有意思，但更吸引我的，是它的写作方式。基于讲稿而成的书，我是第一次读到。

什么时候我也能就某个话题写一本"十讲"呢？这个念头转瞬而逝，但它出现的那个瞬间无比清晰。

毕了业，进了高校，有了一方小小的讲台，教了一届又一届的学生。年岁日长，而学生永远年轻，会在不经意中发觉教学生命终是有限，也不时忆起那个清晰的瞬间。

2021年春季学期每周清晨去怀柔雁栖湖校区上课的班车上，我完成了这本书的初稿。用安·拉莫特在《关于写作：一只鸟接着一只鸟》中的话说，那是不能见人的"拙劣的初稿"。第一轮修改在2021年10月24日至2022年6月11日间，共计200天；2022年的暑假我断断续续完成了第二轮的修改；最后一轮修改自2022年10月10日开始，到2022年12月31日止。历经两载春秋，完成了十年前的小小梦想。

2021年春季学期学术写作课的二十余位学生，是这本书最早的读者。我每修改完一讲，就发给他们阅读，请他们提意见。参考他们的意见，我改进了讲解不到位的内容，换掉了不典型的例子，修改了不流畅的语句和不规范的格式。特别感谢宋波和陈少康两位同学，他们在反馈书稿时，还不时附上自己学科的论文和其他写作资源供我参考。

成书的过程中，我遇到了不少难题，发出了一些求助信。第二讲中关于惠更斯文中"somebody"的指代，我问了不少学物理、学光学的学生，都没有得到确切的答案。几经辗转，才知道这是一个"科学史"的问题。国科大科协的吴宝俊老师帮我联系了研究牛顿的专家——中国科学院自然科学史研究所的樊小龙老师。樊老师热情地回答了我的问题，涉及的背景知识也帮我做了梳理；书稿中一些译自日语、法语、德语的段落，我的同事马潇潇、王昕彦和孙瑾琳老师帮助我做了查证和校对的工作。

历时最长的第一轮修改中，我每日记录书稿的修改进展，以及每日约2.5公里的跑步路线。我跑得很慢，只比走路快一点点。书稿的修改也很慢，匹配了跑步的速度。修改记录有时很长，像个小作文，更多的时候很短，只有寥寥片语。每日记录一点点，我坚信过程本身就是意义。

完成每日的修改记录后，有时也会多写几句。2022年3月21日，东航MU5735发生空难。在如此类的生死时刻，会疑惑自己的专业和平日的工作到底有几分价值。在我的一条朋友圈下，学生留言道：

  老师，我觉得您的课很有用。虽然英语不能像学医学或者心理学能到一线参与救助，但是有可能参与的是您的学生呀。上您课的学生里，有研究量子力学的，有研究计算机的，有研究航天器的，有研究干细胞的，还有我（做生物多样性和生态学）。我们在自己的领域做好螺丝钉，也是一股小小的力量吧！

  这样温暖的鼓励，还有很多很多。感谢关心、帮助、支持我的师长、同事、学生、朋友和家人。

  感谢中国科学院大学对本书出版的资助。感谢许宏晨教授为本书作序。感谢本书责编朱房煦老师。

  我将继续努力，做好一颗螺丝钉。

杜 垚
2022 年岁末